Ninja Foodi 2-Basket Air Fryer Cookbook for Beginners

2000 Days of Quick and Delicious Ninja Dual Air Fryer Recipes Cooking for a Blissful and Healthy Culinary Experience!

Niola Dargrave

Table of Contents

INTRODUCTION

What is Ninja Foodi 2-Basket Air Fryer?

The Ninja Foodi 2-Basket Air Fryer is a versatile kitchen appliance designed to revolutionize the way you cook by combining the functionality of an air fryer with the convenience of having two independent cooking baskets. Manufactured by Ninja, a brand known for innovative kitchen solutions, this particular model is the 6-in-1 8-qt. 2-Basket Air Fryer with Dual Zone Technology.

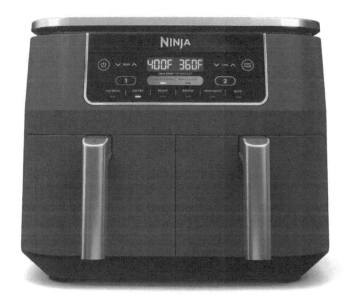

- Design and Capacity:

  The 2-Basket Air Fryer features a sleek and modern design with a user-friendly control panel. Its 8-quart capacity is notably spacious, allowing you to prepare larger quantities of food at once, making it suitable for families or gatherings. The inclusion of two independent baskets is a standout feature, enabling you to cook two different foods simultaneously without compromising on flavor or texture.

- Dual Zone Technology:

  One of the key highlights of this appliance is the Dual Zone Technology. Unlike traditional single-basket air fryers that require you to cook foods back-to-back, this technology offers the flexibility of preparing two distinct dishes simultaneously. The Smart Finish feature, an integral part of Dual Zone Technology, ensures that both foods finish cooking at the same time, eliminating the need for complex timing adjustments.

- Versatile Cooking Programs:

  The Ninja Foodi 2-Basket Air Fryer boasts six versatile cooking programs, catering to a wide range of culinary preferences. These programs include Air Fry, Air Broil, Roast, Bake, Reheat, and Dehydrate. Each setting is tailored to deliver optimal results, whether you're aiming for crispy air-fried delights, succulent roasts, or perfectly baked goods. The appliance's ability to tackle various cooking techniques adds to its appeal, making it a comprehensive solution for diverse culinary needs.

- Easy Maintenance:

  Cleaning up after cooking is often a concern for many, but the Ninja Foodi 2-Basket Air Fryer addresses this with ease. The baskets are designed for easy cleaning, and they can be conveniently washed either in the dishwasher or by hand. This feature enhances the overall user experience, reducing the time and effort spent on post-cooking cleanup.

- User-Friendly Controls:

  Navigating the cooking process is simplified through the intuitive control panel. The inclusion of a Match Cook button allows you to effortlessly copy settings across zones, maximizing the 8-qt capacity without compromising on the quality of the dishes. This level of user-friendly design ensures that both novice and experienced cooks can utilize the appliance to its full potential.

- Smart Cooking Options:

  The Smart Finish feature, enabled by Dual Zone Technology, showcases the appliance's intelligent capabilities. This technology takes the guesswork out of coordinating cooking times, ensuring that both items in the dual baskets are perfectly cooked and ready to be served simultaneously. This not only streamlines the cooking process but also enhances the efficiency of meal preparation.

- Quality Construction:

  Ninja is known for producing high-quality kitchen appliances, and the 2-Basket Air Fryer is no exception. The robust construction, reliable performance, and attention to detail in design contribute to its overall durability and longevity. The incorporation of advanced technology showcases Ninja's commitment to providing cutting-edge solutions for home cooks.

In summary, the Ninja Foodi 2-Basket Air Fryer is a sophisticated kitchen appliance that goes beyond the capabilities of traditional air fryers. With its dual-zone technology, versatile cooking programs, user-friendly controls, and smart cooking options, it offers a comprehensive solution for those seeking efficiency and flexibility in their culinary endeavors. The appliance's thoughtful design and quality construction make it a valuable addition to any kitchen, promising a convenient and enjoyable cooking experience.

Why You Need Such an Appliance at Home

The Ninja Foodi 2-Basket Air Fryer addresses several key reasons why it's a valuable addition to your kitchen.

- Time Efficiency:

  One of the primary advantages of this appliance is its ability to cook two different foods simultaneously. Traditional air fryers require sequential cooking, which can be time-consuming. With the Ninja Foodi 2-Basket Air Fryer, you can prepare a main course and side dish at the same time, reducing overall cooking time.

- Versatility:

  The six cooking programs, including air frying, broiling, roasting, baking, reheating, and dehydrating, provide a wide range of culinary options. Whether you want to make crispy fries, roast a chicken, or dehydrate your favorite fruits, this appliance has you covered.

- Efficient Meal Preparation:

The Smart Finish feature of the Dual Zone Technology ensures that both baskets finish cooking simultaneously. This means you can prepare complete meals without worrying about one dish getting cold while waiting for the other to cook.

- Healthier Cooking:

Air frying is known for its ability to produce crispy and delicious results without the need for excessive oil. The Ninja Foodi 2-Basket Air Fryer allows you to enjoy your favorite fried foods with significantly less oil, promoting a healthier cooking method.

- Convenience:

The dishwasher-safe baskets and easy-to-use controls enhance the overall convenience of this appliance. After cooking, you can simply place the baskets in the dishwasher for hassle-free cleanup.

- Space Saving:

By combining two independent cooking zones in a single appliance, the Ninja Foodi 2-Basket Air Fryer saves valuable counter space compared to having two separate appliances. This is particularly beneficial for those with smaller kitchens.

- Cooking Creativity:

Having the ability to cook two different dishes simultaneously opens up possibilities for experimenting with new recipes and flavor combinations. It encourages culinary creativity and allows you to explore diverse cooking styles without the constraints of a single-basket air fryer.

In summary, the Ninja Foodi 2-Basket Air Fryer is a kitchen appliance that offers time efficiency, versatility, efficient meal preparation, healthier cooking options, convenience, space-saving design, and the opportunity to unleash your cooking creativity.

Cooking Functions and Features

The Ninja Foodi 2-Basket Air Fryer boasts an array of cooking functions and features that cater to diverse culinary needs.

- Air Fry:

Air frying is a standout feature of this appliance. It uses hot air circulation

to cook food, creating a crispy outer layer without submerging the food in oil. This results in a healthier alternative to traditional frying methods while maintaining the desired texture and taste.

- Air Broil:

  The air broil function is ideal for achieving a broiling effect. By using high heat from the top heating element, this feature quickly sears and browns the surface of meats, vegetables, or other dishes, enhancing flavors and textures.

- Roast:

  The roast function evenly cooks food by surrounding it with hot air. This ensures that meats are succulent and flavorful, and vegetables are perfectly roasted. The Ninja Foodi 2-Basket Air Fryer simplifies the roasting process, providing consistent results with minimal effort.

- Bake:

  Equipped with convection baking capabilities, this appliance allows you to bake a variety of dishes, from cookies to casseroles. The even distribution of heat ensures that baked goods are cooked to perfection, with a golden-brown exterior and a moist interior.

- Reheat:

  The reheating function is designed to efficiently warm up leftovers without compromising their original texture or flavor. This is particularly useful for maintaining the quality of previously cooked meals, giving them a fresh-from-the-oven feel.

- Dehydrate:

  The dehydrate function removes moisture from foods, making it easy to create homemade snacks like dried fruits, vegetables, or jerky. This feature adds a new dimension to the appliance, allowing users to experiment with dehydrated culinary creations.

- Dual Zone Technology:

  The standout feature of the Ninja Foodi 2-Basket Air Fryer is its Dual Zone Technology. This innovative technology introduces two independent cooking zones, each equipped with its own basket. Users can choose between the Smart Finish feature and the Match Cook button.

- Smart Finish Feature:

  The Smart Finish feature intelligently manages the cooking process in

both zones, ensuring that the two foods finish cooking at the same time. This eliminates the need for staggered cooking times and allows users to prepare complete meals with ease.

- Match Cook Button:

  The Match Cook button simplifies the cooking process by enabling users to copy settings from one zone to another. This is particularly useful when cooking a large quantity of the same dish, maximizing the 8-quart capacity for a single recipe.

- Versatility in Cooking Capacity:

  With two 8-quart baskets, the Ninja Foodi 2-Basket Air Fryer provides a total cooking capacity of 16 quarts. This generous capacity accommodates large meals, making it suitable for families or gatherings. The ability to cook two different foods simultaneously enhances its versatility.

- User-Friendly Controls:

  The appliance features user-friendly controls that make it easy to select cooking functions, set temperatures, and adjust cooking times. The intuitive interface ensures that both novice and experienced cooks can navigate the settings with ease.

- Dishwasher-Safe Baskets:

  For added convenience, the cooking baskets are dishwasher-safe. This simplifies the cleaning process, allowing users to easily maintain the hygiene of the appliance. However, for those who prefer handwashing, the baskets are designed to be cleaned manually as well.

In conclusion, the Ninja Foodi 2-Basket Air Fryer excels in providing a wide range of cooking functions and features. From air frying to dehydrating, the appliance is designed to cater to diverse culinary preferences, offering a convenient and versatile solution for home cooks. The integration of Dual Zone Technology further enhances its capabilities, making it a standout choice in the realm of air fryers.

Cleaning and Maintenance

Maintaining your Ninja Foodi 6-in-1 8-qt. 2-Basket Air Fryer with Dual Zone Technology is essential for ensuring optimal performance and longevity. Regular cleaning and proper maintenance will not only keep your appliance in top condition but also contribute to the overall safety of its use.

- Exterior Cleaning:

  Start by unplugging the appliance and allowing it to cool down. Wipe the exterior with a damp cloth to remove any splatters or stains. For stubborn stains, a mixture of mild detergent and water can be used. Avoid using abrasive cleaners or scouring pads, as they may damage the finish.

- Basket and Crisper Plate:

  The baskets and crisper plate are likely to accumulate oil and food residues after each use. These components are dishwasher-safe, making cleanup convenient. Alternatively, you can hand wash them with warm, soapy water. Ensure thorough drying before reinserting them into the appliance.

It's essential to clean these components promptly to prevent the buildup of grease, which can affect the air frying performance.

- Interior Cleaning:

The interior of the air fryer may also accumulate grease and food particles. To clean it, use a damp cloth or sponge with mild detergent. Ensure that the appliance is unplugged and cooled down before cleaning the interior. If there are any stubborn residues, you can use a soft brush or toothbrush to gently scrub them away.

- Heating Element and Fan:

Avoid direct contact with the heating element and fan, as they can be damaged easily. Wipe the heating element and fan area with a damp cloth if needed, being careful not to apply excessive pressure. Ensure that no food particles or debris are blocking the fan, as this can affect the air circulation.

- Control Panel and Housing:

Gently wipe the control panel and housing with a soft, damp cloth. Be cautious not to let water seep into the control panel. If needed, you can use a mild cleaning solution suitable for electronics. Always ensure that the appliance is completely dry before plugging it in.

- Smart Finish Feature and DualZone Technology:

The Smart Finish feature and DualZone Technology contribute to the unique functionality of this air fryer. While these components don't require separate cleaning, it's essential to follow the manufacturer's guidelines for maintenance. Regularly check for any signs of wear or damage to ensure the proper functioning of these advanced features.

General Maintenance Tips:

Always refer to the user manual for specific cleaning instructions and maintenance guidelines.

Regularly inspect the power cord for any signs of wear or damage. If any issues are detected, contact the manufacturer for replacement or repair.

Store the air fryer in a cool, dry place when not in use to prevent dust accumulation and potential damage.

By incorporating these cleaning and maintenance practices into your routine, you can enjoy efficient and safe cooking with your Ninja Foodi 2-Basket Air Fryer for years to come.

Common Problems & Troubleshooting Guide

Even with a high-quality appliance like the Ninja Foodi 6-in-1 8-qt. 2-Basket Air Fryer, occasional issues may arise. Understanding common problems and having

a troubleshooting guide can help you address these issues efficiently, ensuring uninterrupted use of your air fryer.

- Uneven Cooking:

  If you notice that your food is not cooking evenly, it could be due to improper placement or overcrowding in the baskets. Ensure that you distribute food evenly in the baskets, allowing proper air circulation. Avoid overcrowding to ensure each item receives consistent heat. Additionally, rotating or flipping the food during cooking can help achieve more uniform results.

- Food Not Crispy:

  If your air-fried food is not achieving the desired crispiness, it may be due to excessive moisture. Patting food dry before placing it in the baskets can help. Additionally, make sure the baskets are not overcrowded, as this can lead to steaming rather than crisping. Preheating the air fryer before adding food can also contribute to a crispier texture.

- Smoke Emission:

Excessive smoke during cooking may result from oil or food residue on the heating element. Ensure the air fryer is clean, especially the interior and heating element area. If using oil, use it sparingly to avoid smoke. If smoke persists, check the oil quality, as some oils have lower smoke points.

- Error Messages on the Display:

  If the control panel displays an error message, consult the user manual for guidance. Error messages may indicate issues with temperature sensors, fan malfunctions, or other technical problems. Unplug the appliance, wait for a few minutes, and then plug it back in to see if the error clears. If the issue persists, contact the manufacturer's customer support for further assistance.

- Unusual Noises:

  While some noise is normal during air frying due to the fan and heating element, unusual or loud noises may indicate a problem. Check for any loose components or foreign objects inside the air fryer. If the noise persists, it's advisable to contact the manufacturer for professional inspection and repair.

- Appliance Not Turning On:

  If your air fryer doesn't turn on, check if it's properly plugged into a functioning power outlet. Ensure that the power cord is not damaged. If the issue persists, try plugging the appliance into a different outlet to rule out electrical issues. If the problem continues, contact customer support for assistance.

- Smart Finish and DualZone Technology Not Functioning:

  If the Smart Finish feature or DualZone Technology is not working as expected, ensure that you are following the correct procedures as outlined in the user manual. Check for any error messages on the display. If the problem persists, it may require professional inspection to diagnose and address technical issues.

- Odor Retention:

  If your air fryer retains food odors, clean the interior thoroughly, including the baskets and crisper plate. Consider placing a small bowl of baking soda inside the air fryer when not in use to absorb lingering odors. If the issue persists, contact the manufacturer for additional guidance.

In conclusion, being aware of these common problems and their troubleshooting solutions empowers you to address issues promptly and enjoy a seamless cooking experience with your Ninja Foodi 2-Basket Air Fryer. Regular maintenance and adherence to usage guidelines contribute to the longevity and performance of your appliance. If problems persist, don't hesitate to seek assistance from the manufacturer's customer support for professional guidance and resolution.

Chapter 1: Breakfast

Air-Baked Cinnamon Roll Twists

Prep Time: 15 Minutes   Cook Time: 12 Minutes   Serves: 4

Ingredients:

- 1 can refrigerated cinnamon roll dough
- 2 tablespoons melted butter
- 1/4 cup brown sugar
- 1 teaspoon ground cinnamon
- Cream cheese icing (included with the cinnamon roll dough)

Directions:

1. Set one basket to bake at 350°F for 5 minutes.
2. Unroll the cinnamon roll dough and separate it into individual rolls.
3. Twist each roll and place them in the first basket.
4. Brush the twisted rolls with melted butter.
5. In a small bowl, mix brown sugar and ground cinnamon.
6. Sprinkle the cinnamon sugar mixture over the twisted rolls.
7. Bake the cinnamon roll twists for 10-12 minutes until they are golden brown.
8. Set the second basket to air fry at 375°F for 5 minutes.
9. Place the second basket with the preheated air fry setting and cook breakfast sausages until browned.
10. Press the Smart Finish button.
11. Once baked, remove the twists from the first basket.
12. Ice the warm twists with cream cheese icing.
13. Enjoy.

Nutritional Value (Amount per Serving):

Calories: 151; Fat: 8.71; Carb: 18.13; Protein: 0.98

Breakfast Pizza

Prep Time: 15 Minutes   Cook Time: 10 Minutes   Serves: 4

Ingredients:

- 1 pre-cooked pizza crust
- 1/2 cup marinara sauce
- 1 cup shredded mozzarella cheese
- 1/2 cup cooked sausage, crumbled
- 1/4 cup sliced bell peppers
- 1/4 cup sliced mushrooms
- 4 large eggs
- Salt and pepper to taste
- Fresh basil for garnish

Directions:

1. Set one basket to reheat at 350°F for 5 minutes.

2. Spread marinara sauce over the pre-cooked pizza crust.
3. Sprinkle with mozzarella cheese, crumbled sausage, bell peppers, and mushrooms.
4. Place the assembled pizza in the first basket.
5. Reheat for 8-10 minutes or until the cheese is melted and the crust is crispy.
6. Set the second basket to air fry at 375°F for 5 minutes.
7. Crack eggs onto a cooking sheet in the second basket.
8. Air fry for 3-5 minutes until the whites are set but the yolks are still runny.
9. Press the Smart Finish button.
10. Once reheated, remove the pizza from the first basket.
11. Slide the sunny-side-up eggs onto the pizza.
12. Garnish with salt, pepper, and fresh basil.
13. Serve slices of reheated breakfast pizza with runny eggs on top.

Nutritional Value (Amount per Serving):

Calories: 419; Fat: 31.47; Carb: 8.36; Protein: 26.46

Dehydrated Apple Chips and Nut Parfait

Prep Time: 20 Minutes   Cook Time: 3 Hours   Serves: 4

Ingredients:

- 2 apples, thinly sliced
- 1 tablespoon lemon juice
- 1 cup Greek yogurt
- 1/4 cup honey
- 1/2 cup granola
- 1/4 cup chopped nuts (e.g., almonds, walnuts)
- Cinnamon for dusting

Directions:

1. Set one basket to dehydrate at 135°F for 5 minutes.
2. Toss thinly sliced apples in lemon juice to prevent browning.
3. Arrange the apple slices on the dehydrator trays in the first basket.
4. Dehydrate the apple slices for 2-3 hours until they are crispy.
5. In a bowl, mix Greek yogurt with honey.
6. Layer dehydrated apple chips, granola, and chopped nuts in serving glasses.
7. Once dehydrated, remove the apple chips from the first basket.
8. Top the parfait with a dusting of cinnamon.
9. Savor the delightful dehydrated apple chip and nut parfait.

Nutritional Value (Amount per Serving):

Calories: 336; Fat: 12.51; Carb: 49.94; Protein: 9.65

Baked Blueberry Pancake Squares

Prep Time: 15 Minutes   Cook Time: 18 Minutes   Serves: 4

Ingredients:

- 1 cup pancake mix
- 1/2 cup milk
- 1 large egg
- 1 tablespoon melted butter
- 1 cup fresh blueberries
- Maple syrup for serving

Directions:

1. Set one basket to bake at 375°F for 5 minutes.
2. In a bowl, whisk together pancake mix, milk, egg, and melted butter until smooth.
3. Gently fold in fresh blueberries into the pancake batter.
4. Pour the batter into a greased baking pan that fits into the first basket.
5. Place the pan in the first basket and bake for 15-18 minutes until the pancake is golden brown.
6. Set the second basket to air fry at 375°F for 5 minutes.
7. Place breakfast sausages in the second basket and air fry until browned and cooked through.
8. Press the Smart Finish button.
9. Slice the baked pancake into squares.
10. Serve with maple syrup.

Nutritional Value (Amount per Serving):

Calories: 288; Fat: 5.75; Carb: 54.49; Protein: 6.57

Air-Fried Breakfast Burrito Bowl

Prep Time: 20 Minutes   Cook Time: 15 Minutes   Serves: 4

Ingredients:

- 1 cup cooked quinoa or rice
- 1 cup black beans, drained and rinsed
- 1 cup corn kernels (fresh or frozen)
- 1 cup diced tomatoes
- 1/2 cup diced red onions
- 1/2 cup chopped cilantro
- 1 teaspoon ground cumin
- 1 teaspoon chili powder
- Salt and pepper to taste
- 4 large eggs

Directions:

1. Set one basket to air fry at 375°F for 5 minutes.
2. In a bowl, mix together cooked quinoa or rice, black beans, corn, diced tomatoes, red onions, cilantro, ground cumin, chili powder, salt, and pepper.
3. Transfer the burrito bowl mixture into the first basket.

4. Air fry for 12-15 minutes, stirring occasionally, until the ingredients are heated through and slightly crispy.
5. At the same time, set the second basket to bake at 350°F for 5 minutes.
6. Crack eggs into the second basket.
7. Bake for 5-7 minutes until the egg whites are set but the yolks are still runny.
8. Press the Smart Finish button.
9. Spoon the air-fried burrito bowl into serving bowls.
10. Top with baked eggs and additional cilantro if desired.
11. Enjoy a flavorful and protein-packed breakfast with this air-fried breakfast burrito bowl!

Nutritional Value (Amount per Serving):

Calories: 255; Fat: 11.79; Carb: 36.14; Protein: 12.33

Reheated Breakfast Hash

Prep Time: 15 Minutes   Cook Time: 12 Minutes   Serves: 4

Ingredients:

- 1 pound cooked and diced potatoes (leftover or pre-cooked)
- 1/2 cup diced bell peppers (assorted colors)
- 1/2 cup diced onions
- 1/2 cup cooked and crumbled sausage
- 1/2 cup shredded cheddar cheese
- 4 large eggs
- Salt and pepper to taste
- Chopped green onions for garnish

Directions:

1. Set one basket to reheat at 375°F for 5 minutes.
2. In a bowl, combine diced potatoes, diced bell peppers, diced onions, crumbled sausage, and shredded cheddar cheese.
3. Transfer the hash mixture into the first basket.
4. Reheat for 10-12 minutes, stirring occasionally, until the hash is heated through and the edges are crispy.
5. At the same time, set the second basket to air fry at 375°F for 5 minutes.
6. Crack eggs into the second basket.
7. Air fry for 5-7 minutes until the egg whites are set but the yolks are still runny.
8. Press the Smart Finish button.
9. Spoon the reheated breakfast hash onto plates.
10. Top with sunny-side-up eggs and garnish with chopped green onions.

11. Relish a comforting and hearty breakfast with reheated breakfast hash and perfectly cooked eggs.

Nutritional Value (Amount per Serving):

Calories: 336; Fat: 12.41; Carb: 43.11; Protein: 15.68

Air-Fried Breakfast BLT Wraps

Prep Time: 15 Minutes   Cook Time: 12 Minutes   Serves: 4

Ingredients:

- 4 large flour tortillas
- 1 cup cherry tomatoes, halved
- 1 cup lettuce, shredded
- 8 slices bacon, cooked until crispy
- 4 large eggs
- Salt and pepper to taste
- Mayonnaise for spreading

Directions:

1. Set one basket to air fry at 375°F for 5 minutes.
2. Lay out the flour tortillas and spread a thin layer of mayonnaise on each.
3. Divide shredded lettuce, halved cherry tomatoes, and crispy bacon slices among the tortillas.
4. Fold the tortillas into wraps.
5. Place the wraps in the first basket and air fry for 8-10 minutes until they are golden brown and crispy.
6. At the same time, set the second basket to bake at 350°F for 5 minutes.
7. Crack eggs into the second basket.
8. Bake for 5-7 minutes until the egg whites are set but the yolks are still runny.
9. Press the Smart Finish button.
10. Once air-fried, remove the BLT wraps from the first basket.
11. Top each wrap with a sunny-side-up egg.
12. Relish these delicious and crunchy Air-Fried Breakfast BLT Wraps with runny eggs!

Nutritional Value (Amount per Serving):

Calories: 416; Fat: 28.15; Carb: 26.83; Protein: 13.45

Dehydrated Berry Yogurt Parfait

Prep Time: 20 Minutes   Cook Time: 3 Hours   Serves: 4

Ingredients:

- 2 cups mixed berries (strawberries, blueberries, raspberries)

- 2 cups Greek yogurt
- 1/4 cup honey
- 1 cup granola
- 1/4 cup chopped almonds
- Mint leaves for garnish

Directions:

1. Set one basket to dehydrate at 135°F for 5 minutes.
2. In a bowl, mix together Greek yogurt and honey.
3. Layer the bottom of the cooking trays with a thin layer of the yogurt mixture.
4. Place the mixed berries on top of the yogurt layer in the first basket.
5. Dehydrate the berries and yogurt for 2-3 hours until the berries are shriveled and the yogurt is firm.
6. At the same time, set the second basket to air fry at 375°F for 5 minutes.
7. Spread granola and chopped almonds in the second basket.
8. Air fry for 5-7 minutes until the granola is golden and almonds are roasted.
9. Press the Smart Finish button.
10. Once dehydrated, remove the berry yogurt parfait from the first basket.
11. Layer the dehydrated berries and yogurt with air-fried granola and almonds in serving glasses.
12. Garnish with mint leaves.

Nutritional Value (Amount per Serving):

Calories: 766; Fat: 33.85; Carb: 97.6; Protein: 20.35

Reheated Sweet Potato Hash Browns

Prep Time: 15 Minutes   Cook Time: 12 Minutes   Serves: 4

Ingredients:

- 2 large sweet potatoes, peeled and grated
- 1/2 cup diced red bell peppers
- 1/2 cup diced red onions
- 1 teaspoon smoked paprika
- 1/2 teaspoon garlic powder
- Salt and pepper to taste
- 4 large eggs
- Chopped parsley for garnish

Directions:

1. Set one basket to reheat at 375°F for 5 minutes.
2. In a bowl, mix grated sweet potatoes, diced red bell peppers, diced red onions, smoked paprika, garlic powder, salt, and pepper.
3. Transfer the sweet potato mixture into the first basket.

4. Reheat for 10-12 minutes, stirring occasionally, until the hash browns are heated through and crispy.
5. At the same time, set the second basket to air fry at 375°F for 5 minutes.
6. Crack eggs into the second basket.
7. Air fry for 5-7 minutes until the egg whites are set but the yolks are still runny.
8. Press the Smart Finish button.
9. Spoon the reheated sweet potato hash browns onto plates.
10. Top with sunny-side-up eggs and garnish with chopped parsley.

Nutritional Value (Amount per Serving):

Calories: 157; Fat: 4.89; Carb: 23.74; Protein: 5.59

Air-Fried Veggie Omelette

Prep Time: 15 Minutes   Cook Time: 12 Minutes   Serves: 4

Ingredients:

- 8 large eggs
- 1/2 cup diced bell peppers (assorted colors)
- 1/2 cup diced tomatoes
- 1/4 cup diced red onions
- 1/2 cup chopped spinach
- 1/2 cup shredded cheddar cheese
- Salt and pepper to taste
- Cooking spray

Directions:

1. Set one basket to air fry at 375°F for 5 minutes.
2. In a bowl, whisk together eggs, diced bell peppers, diced tomatoes, diced red onions, chopped spinach, shredded cheddar cheese, salt, and pepper.
3. Spray the air fryer basket with cooking spray.
4. Pour the omelette mixture into the first basket.
5. Air fry for 10-12 minutes, pausing to gently lift the edges with a spatula to allow uncooked eggs to flow to the edges, until the omelette is set and the edges are golden.
6. At the same time, set the second basket to bake at 350°F for 5 minutes.
7. Toss diced potatoes with olive oil, salt, and pepper.
8. Bake in the second basket until golden and crispy.
9. Press the Smart Finish button.
10. Slide the air-fried omelette onto a serving plate.
11. Serve with a side of crispy baked breakfast potatoes.

Nutritional Value (Amount per Serving):

Calories: 175; Fat: 11.64; Carb: 7.65; Protein: 9.93

Baked Apple Cinnamon French Toast

Prep Time: 20 Minutes   Cook Time: 25 Minutes   Serves: 4

Ingredients:

- 8 slices of bread, cubed
- 2 apples, peeled and diced
- 4 large eggs
- 1 cup milk
- 1/4 cup maple syrup
- 1 teaspoon ground cinnamon
- 4 bacon strips
- 1/2 teaspoon vanilla extract
- 1/2 cup chopped pecans or walnuts (optional)
- Powdered sugar for dusting

Directions:

1. Set one basket to bake at 375°F for 5 minutes.
2. In a bowl, whisk together eggs, milk, maple syrup, ground cinnamon, and vanilla extract.
3. Place cubed bread and diced apples in the first basket.
4. Pour the egg mixture over the bread and apples, ensuring even coating.
5. Bake for 20-25 minutes until the French toast is golden and cooked through.
6. At the same time, set the second basket to air fry at 375°F for 5 minutes.
7. Lay bacon strips in the second basket and air fry until crispy.
8. Press the Smart Finish button.
9. Remove the baked French toast from the first basket.
10. Serve with a side of crispy air-fried bacon.

Nutritional Value (Amount per Serving):

Calories: 385; Fat: 16.01; Carb: 52.39; Protein: 10.49

Reheated Breakfast Enchiladas

Prep Time: 20 Minutes   Cook Time: 15 Minutes   Serves: 4

Ingredients:

- 8 small flour tortillas
- 1 cup cooked and shredded chicken
- 1/2 cup black beans, drained and rinsed
- 1/2 cup diced tomatoes
- 1/4 cup diced red onions
- 1 cup shredded Mexican cheese blend
- 1 cup enchilada sauce
- 4 large eggs
- Fresh cilantro for garnish

Directions:

1. Set one basket to reheat at 375°F for 5 minutes.
2. In a tortilla, layer shredded chicken, black beans, diced tomatoes, red onions, and shredded cheese.
3. Roll up the tortilla and place it seam-side down in the first basket.
4. Reheat for 12-15 minutes until the enchiladas are heated through and the cheese is melted.
5. At the same time, set the second basket to air fry at 375°F for 5 minutes.
6. Crack eggs into the second basket.
7. Air fry for 5-7 minutes until the egg whites are set but the yolks are still runny.
8. Press the Smart Finish button.
9. Remove the reheated enchiladas from the first basket.
10. Top each enchilada with a sunny-side-up egg and garnish with fresh cilantro.

Nutritional Value (Amount per Serving):

Calories: 667; Fat: 32.95; Carb: 63.49; Protein: 28.26

Air-Fried Avocado and Egg Breakfast Tacos

Prep Time: 15 Minutes   Cook Time: 10 Minutes   Serves: 4

Ingredients:

- 4 small flour tortillas
- 2 ripe avocados, sliced
- 4 large eggs
- Salt and pepper to taste
- Salsa for topping
- 1 frozen hash browns
- Fresh cilantro for garnish

Directions:

1. Set one basket to air fry at 375°F for 5 minutes.
2. Press the Smart Finish button.
3. Place tortillas in the first basket.
4. Arrange avocado slices on each tortilla.
5. Crack one egg onto each tortilla, on top of the avocado slices.
6. Sprinkle with salt and pepper.
7. Air fry for 8-10 minutes until the egg whites are set but the yolks are still runny.
8. At the same time, set the second basket to bake at 350°F for 5 minutes.
9. Spread frozen hash browns in the second basket and bake until crispy.
10. Press the Smart Finish button.
11. Remove the avocado and egg tacos from the first basket.
12. Serve with a side of crispy hash browns, topped with salsa and garnished

with fresh cilantro.

Nutritional Value (Amount per Serving):

Calories: 459; Fat: 27.48; Carb: 47.11; Protein: 9.91

Baked Banana Bread Oatmeal

Prep Time: 15 Minutes   Cook Time: 25 Minutes   Serves: 4

Ingredients:

- 2 cups old-fashioned oats
- 2 ripe bananas, mashed
- 1/2 cup chopped nuts (e.g., walnuts or pecans)
- 1/4 cup honey or maple syrup
- 2 cups milk (dairy or plant-based)
- 2 large eggs
- 4 bacon strips
- 1 teaspoon vanilla extract
- 1 teaspoon ground cinnamon
- 1/2 teaspoon baking powder
- Pinch of salt
- Sliced bananas for topping

Directions:

1. Set one basket to bake at 375°F for 5 minutes.
2. In a bowl, mix together oats, mashed bananas, chopped nuts, honey or maple syrup, milk, eggs, vanilla extract, ground cinnamon, baking powder, and a pinch of salt.
3. Pour the oat mixture into a greased baking dish that fits into the first basket.
4. Bake for 20-25 minutes until the edges are golden and the center is set.
5. At the same time, set the second basket to air fry at 375°F for 5 minutes.
6. Lay bacon strips in the second basket and air fry until crispy.
7. Press the Smart Finish button.
8. Remove the baked banana bread oatmeal from the first basket.
9. Serve slices with a side of crispy air-fried bacon and sliced bananas.

Nutritional Value (Amount per Serving):

Calories: 448; Fat: 20.58; Carb: 70.76; Protein: 16.25

Reheated Breakfast Burritos

Prep Time: 20 Minutes   Cook Time: 15 Minutes   Serves: 4

Ingredients:

- 4 large flour tortillas
- 1 cup cooked and shredded hash browns
- 1/2 cup cooked and crumbled breakfast sausage
- 1/2 cup shredded cheddar cheese
- 4 large eggs, scrambled
- 4 bacon strips
- Salt and pepper to taste
- Salsa and guacamole for serving

Directions:

1. Set one basket to reheat at 375°F for 5 minutes.
2. Lay out tortillas and divide hash browns, crumbled breakfast sausage, shredded cheddar cheese, and scrambled eggs among them.
3. Place the assembled burritos in the first basket.
4. Reheat for 12-15 minutes until the burritos are heated through and the edges are crispy.
5. At the same time, set the second basket to air fry at 375°F for 5 minutes.
6. Lay bacon strips in the second basket and air fry until crispy.
7. Press the Smart Finish button.
8. Remove the reheated breakfast burritos from the first basket.
9. Serve with a side of crispy air-fried bacon, salsa, and guacamole.

Nutritional Value (Amount per Serving):

Calories: 433; Fat: 19.44; Carb: 44.33; Protein: 21.19

Dehydrated Mango and Yogurt Parfait

Prep Time: 20 Minutes   Cook Time: 4 Hours   Serves: 4

Ingredients:

- 2 ripe mangoes, peeled and diced
- 1 tablespoon lemon juice
- 2 cups Greek yogurt
- 1/4 cup honey
- 1 cup granola
- 1 cup almonds
- 1/4 cup shredded coconut
- Mint leaves for garnish

Directions:

1. Set one basket to dehydrate at 135°F for 5 minutes.
2. Toss diced mangoes in lemon juice to prevent browning.
3. Arrange mango slices on dehydrator trays in the first basket
4. Dehydrate mango slices for 3-4 hours until they are chewy and slightly dried.
5. At the same time, set the second basket to air fry at 375°F for 5 minutes.

6. Spread almonds in the second basket and air fry until roasted.
7. Press the Smart Finish button.
8. In serving glasses, layer Greek yogurt, dehydrated mango slices, granola, and toasted almonds.
9. Top the parfait with shredded coconut.
10. Garnish with mint leaves.

Nutritional Value (Amount per Serving):

Calories: 419; Fat: 14.31; Carb: 58.39; Protein: 17.23

Air-Fried Veggie Omelette

Prep Time: 10 Minutes   Cook Time: 15 Minutes   Serves: 4

Ingredients:

- 8 large eggs
- 1/2 cup diced bell peppers (assorted colors)
- 1/2 cup diced onions
- 1/2 cup diced tomatoes
- 1/2 cup shredded cheddar cheese
- Salt and pepper to taste

Directions:

1. In a large bowl, beat the eggs until well combined.
2. Season with salt and pepper.
3. In one basket, evenly distribute half of the diced bell peppers, onions, and tomatoes.
4. In the other basket, do the same with the remaining veggies.
5. Carefully pour half of the beaten eggs over the veggies in each basket.
6. Place both baskets in the Ninja Foodi Air Fryer.
7. Press the Match Cook button.
8. Set the air fryer to 350°F and air fry for 12-15 minutes or until the omelette are puffed and golden brown.
9. Sprinkle shredded cheddar cheese over one half of each omelette.
10. Continue cooking for an additional 2-3 minutes until the cheese is melted.
11. Carefully remove the omelette from the baskets.
12. Fold the omelette in half and transfer to a serving plate.
13. Serve hot and enjoy a delicious and fluffy veggie omelette!

Nutritional Value (Amount per Serving):

Calories: 175; Fat: 11.63; Carb: 7.92; Protein: 9.85

Chapter 2: Poultry

Garlic Butter Roasted Whole Chicken with Lemon Herb Potatoes

Prep Time: 20 Minutes   Cook Time: 1 Hour 30 Minutes   Serves: 4-6

Ingredients:

- 1 whole chicken (about 4 lbs)
- 1/2 cup unsalted butter, melted
- 4 cloves garlic, minced
- 1 tablespoon dried thyme
- 1 tablespoon dried rosemary
- Salt and pepper to taste
- 4 large potatoes, diced
- Zest and juice of 1 lemon

Directions:

1. Preheat one side of your Ninja Foodi 2-Basket Air Fryer to Roast at 375°F.
2. In a bowl, mix melted butter, minced garlic, dried thyme, dried rosemary, salt, and pepper.
3. Rub the whole chicken with the garlic butter mixture and place it in one basket.
4. Roast the chicken for 1 hour to 1 hour and 15 minutes, or until the internal temperature reaches 165°F.
5. At the same time, preheat the other side of the Air Fryer to 400°F using the Air Fry function.
6. Toss diced potatoes with olive oil, salt, and pepper.
7. Place the seasoned potatoes in the second basket and air fry for 30-35 minutes, shaking the basket halfway through.
8. Press the Smart Finish button.
9. Sprinkle lemon zest and juice over the roasted chicken and serve with lemon herb potatoes.

Nutritional Value (Amount per Serving):

Calories: 1090; Fat: 38.09; Carb: 125.34; Protein: 65.78

Cajun-Spiced Air-Baked Chicken Tenders with Sweet Potato Fries

Prep Time: 15 Minutes   Cook Time: 25 Minutes   Serves: 4-6

Ingredients:

- 2 lbs chicken tenders
- 2 tablespoons olive oil
- 2 tablespoons Cajun seasoning
- 1 teaspoon garlic powder
- Salt and pepper to taste
- 4 large sweet potatoes, cut into fries

Directions:

1. Preheat one side of your Ninja Foodi 2-Basket Air Fryer to Bake at 375°F.

2. In a bowl, toss chicken tenders with olive oil, Cajun seasoning, garlic powder, salt, and pepper.
3. Place the seasoned chicken tenders in one basket and bake for 15-20 minutes, turning halfway through.
4. At the same time, preheat the other side of the Air Fryer to Air Fry at 400°F.
5. Toss sweet potato fries with olive oil, salt, and pepper.
6. Place the seasoned sweet potato fries in the second basket and air fry for 10-15 minutes.
7. Press the Smart Finish button.
8. Serve Cajun-spiced chicken tenders with a side of crispy sweet potato fries.

Nutritional Value (Amount per Serving):

Calories: 651; Fat: 29.03; Carb: 64.97; Protein: 33

Italian Herb-Stuffed Cornish Hens with Roasted Vegetables

Prep Time: 25 Minutes   Cook Time: 1 Hour   Serves: 4

Ingredients:

- 4 Cornish hens
- 3 tablespoons olive oil
- 2 teaspoons dried Italian herbs (rosemary, thyme, oregano)
- 1 teaspoon garlic powder
- Salt and pepper to taste
- 4 cups mixed vegetables (carrots, bell peppers, zucchini), diced

Directions:

1. Preheat one side of your Ninja Foodi 2-Basket Air Fryer to Roast at 375°F.
2. In a bowl, mix olive oil, dried Italian herbs, garlic powder, salt, and pepper.
3. Stuff each Cornish hen with the herb mixture and place them in one basket.
4. Roast the Cornish hens for 50-55 minutes, turning halfway through, or until the internal temperature reaches 165°F.
5. At the same time, preheat the other side of the Air Fryer to Air Fry at 400°F.
6. Toss mixed vegetables with olive oil, salt, and pepper.
7. Place the seasoned vegetables in the second basket and air fry for 20-25 minutes, shaking the basket halfway through.
8. Press the Smart Finish button.
9. Serve the Italian herb-stuffed Cornish hens with a side of roasted vegetables.

Nutritional Value (Amount per Serving):

Calories: 1303; Fat: 43.74; Carb: 12.51; Protein: 201.82

Pesto-Marinated Turkey Jerky

Prep Time: 15 Minutes   Cook Time: 4-6 Hours   Serves: 4-6

Ingredients

- 1.5 lbs turkey breast, thinly sliced
- 1 cup pesto sauce
- 1 teaspoon onion powder
- 1 teaspoon garlic powder
- 1/2 teaspoon black pepper

Directions:

1. In a bowl, combine turkey slices with pesto sauce, onion powder, garlic powder, and black pepper. Marinate in the refrigerator for at least 2 hours or overnight.
2. Preheat one side of your Ninja Foodi 2-Basket Air Fryer to Dehydrate at 160°F.
3. Arrange marinated turkey slices on dehydrator trays, ensuring they are not touching.
4. Dehydrate for 4-6 hours or until the turkey becomes jerky-like, flipping the slices halfway through.
5. After they are done, switch the Air Fryer to Air Fry at 375°F.
6. Air fry the dehydrated turkey for 5-10 minutes to enhance crispiness.
7. Allow the turkey jerky to cool before serving.

Nutritional Value (Amount per Serving):

Calories: 483; Fat: 36.79; Carb: 3; Protein: 34.81

Honey Mustard Glazed Chicken Drumsticks with Crispy Brussel Sprouts

Prep Time: 20 Minutes   Cook Time: 40 Minutes   Serves: 4-6

Ingredients:

- 2 lbs chicken drumsticks
- 1/4 cup Dijon mustard
- 1/4 cup honey
- 2 tablespoons olive oil
- 1 teaspoon garlic powder
- Salt and pepper to taste
- 1 lb Brussels sprouts, halved

Directions:

1. Preheat one side of your Ninja Foodi 2-Basket Air Fryer to Bake at 375°F.

2. In a bowl, whisk together Dijon mustard, honey, olive oil, garlic powder, salt, and pepper.
3. Coat chicken drumsticks with the honey mustard mixture and place them in one basket.
4. Bake the chicken for 30-35 minutes, turning halfway through, or until the internal temperature reaches 165°F.
5. At the same time, preheat the other side of the Air Fryer to Air Fry at 400°F.
6. Toss Brussels sprouts with olive oil, salt, and pepper.
7. Place the seasoned Brussels sprouts in the second basket and air fry for 15-20 minutes, shaking the basket halfway through.
8. Press the Smart Finish button.
9. Serve honey mustard glazed chicken drumsticks with a side of crispy Brussels sprouts.

Nutritional Value (Amount per Serving):

Calories: 444; Fat: 22.8; Carb: 24.32; Protein: 36.67

Roasted Whole Chicken with Herb-Roasted Potatoes

Prep Time: 25 Minutes   Cook Time: 1 Hour 30 Minutes   Serves: 4-6

Ingredients:

- 1 whole chicken (about 4 lbs)
- 3 tablespoons olive oil
- 2 teaspoons dried Italian herbs (rosemary, thyme, oregano)
- 1 teaspoon garlic powder
- Salt and pepper to taste
- 4 large potatoes, diced

Directions:

1. Preheat one side of your Ninja Foodi 2-Basket Air Fryer to Roast at 375°F.
2. Rub the whole chicken with olive oil, dried Italian herbs, garlic powder, salt, and pepper.
3. Place the chicken in one basket and roast for 1 hour to 1 hour and 15 minutes, turning halfway through, or until the internal temperature reaches 165°F.
4. At the same time, preheat the other side of the Air Fryer to Air Fry at 400°F.
5. Toss diced potatoes with olive oil, salt, and pepper.
6. Place the seasoned potatoes in the second basket and air fry for 30-35 minutes, shaking the basket halfway through.
7. Press the Smart Finish button.

8. Serve the rotisserie-style whole chicken with a side of herb-roasted potatoes.

Nutritional Value (Amount per Serving):

Calories: 1046; Fat: 33.81; Carb: 124.42; Protein: 64.96

Maple Glazed Chicken Thighs with Cinnamon Roasted Butternut Squash

Prep Time: 20 Minutes   Cook Time: 40 Minutes   Serves: 4-6

Ingredients:

- 2 lbs chicken thighs, bone-in, skin-on
- 1/3 cup maple syrup
- 2 tablespoons soy sauce
- 1 teaspoon Dijon mustard
- Salt and pepper to taste
- 1 medium butternut squash, peeled and diced
- 1 tablespoon olive oil
- 1 teaspoon ground cinnamon

Directions:

1. Preheat one side of your Ninja Foodi 2-Basket Air Fryer to Bake at 375°F.
2. In a bowl, mix maple syrup, soy sauce, Dijon mustard, salt, and pepper.
3. Coat chicken thighs with the maple glaze and place them in one basket.
4. Bake the chicken for 25-30 minutes, turning halfway through, or until the internal temperature reaches 175°F.
5. At the same time, preheat the other side of the Air Fryer to Air Fry at 400°F.
6. Toss diced butternut squash with olive oil, salt, and ground cinnamon.
7. Place the seasoned butternut squash in the second basket and air fry for 15-20 minutes, shaking the basket halfway through.
8. Press the Smart Finish button.
9. Serve the maple glazed chicken thighs with a side of cinnamon-roasted butternut squash.

Nutritional Value (Amount per Serving):

Calories: 523; Fat: 34.11; Carb: 22.61; Protein: 31.13

Hawaiian Teriyaki Air-Dehydrated Chicken Jerky

Prep Time: 15 Minutes   Cook Time: 4-6 Hours   Serves: 4

Ingredients:

- 1.5 lbs chicken breast, thinly sliced
- 1 cup teriyaki sauce
- 1 tablespoon pineapple juice
- 1 teaspoon garlic powder
- 1/2 teaspoon ground ginger

Directions:

1. In a bowl, combine chicken slices with teriyaki sauce, pineapple juice, garlic powder, and ground ginger. Marinate in the refrigerator for at least 2 hours or overnight.
2. Preheat one side of your Ninja Foodi 2-Basket Air Fryer to Dehydrate at 160°F.
3. Press the Smart Finish button.
4. Arrange marinated chicken slices in air fryer basket, ensuring they are not touching.
5. Dehydrate for 4-6 hours or until the chicken becomes jerky-like, flipping the slices halfway through.
6. Once done, switch the Air Fryer to Air Fry at 375°F.
7. Air fry the dehydrated chicken for 5-10 minutes to enhance crispiness.
8. Allow the teriyaki chicken jerky to cool before serving.

Nutritional Value (Amount per Serving):

Calories: 362; Fat: 15.77; Carb: 12.44; Protein: 39.9

Mediterranean Herb-Baked Chicken Drumsticks with Greek Salad

Prep Time: 20 Minutes   Cook Time: 40 Minutes   Serves: 4-6

Ingredients:

- 2 lbs chicken drumsticks
- 3 tablespoons olive oil
- 1 tablespoon dried oregano
- 1 teaspoon dried basil
- 1 teaspoon garlic powder
- 1/2 cup feta cheese, crumbled
- Salt and pepper to taste
- 2 cups cherry tomatoes, halved
- 1 cucumber, diced
- 1/2 cup Kalamata olives, sliced

Directions:

1. Preheat one side of your Ninja Foodi 2-Basket Air Fryer to Bake at 375°F.
2. In a bowl, mix olive oil, dried oregano, dried basil, garlic powder, salt, and pepper.
3. Coat chicken drumsticks with the herb mixture and place them in one basket.
4. Bake the chicken for 30-35 minutes, turning halfway through, or until the

internal temperature reaches 175°F.

5. In a separate bowl, combine cherry tomatoes, cucumber, Kalamata olives, and crumbled feta to make the Greek salad.
6. Serve the Mediterranean herb-baked chicken drumsticks with a generous side of Greek salad.

Nutritional Value (Amount per Serving):

Calories: 433; Fat: 29.53; Carb: 4.67; Protein: 35.67

Panko-Crusted Chicken Breast with Roasted Vegetables

Prep Time: 20 Minutes   Cook Time: 35 Minutes   Serves: 4-6

Ingredients:

- 4 boneless, skinless chicken breasts
- 1 cup panko breadcrumbs
- 2 tablespoons grated Parmesan cheese
- 1 teaspoon dried Italian herbs
- Salt and pepper to taste
- 1 lb mixed vegetables (bell peppers, cherry tomatoes, red onion), diced
- 2 tablespoons olive oil

Directions:

1. Preheat one side of your Ninja Foodi 2-Basket Air Fryer to Air Fry at 375°F
2. In a shallow bowl, combine panko breadcrumbs, grated Parmesan cheese, dried Italian herbs, salt, and pepper.
3. Coat each chicken breast with the breadcrumb mixture and place them in one basket.
4. Air fry the chicken for 20-25 minutes, turning halfway through, or until the internal temperature reaches 165°F.
5. At the same time, preheat the other side of the Air Fryer to Air Fry at 400°F.
6. Toss mixed vegetables with olive oil, salt, and pepper.
7. Place the seasoned vegetables in the second basket and air fry for 15-20 minutes, shaking the basket halfway through.
8. Press the Match Cook button.
9. Serve the panko-crusted chicken breasts with a side of roasted vegetables.

Nutritional Value (Amount per Serving):

Calories: 451; Fat: 17.95; Carb: 51.79; Protein: 21.37

Baked BBQ Chicken Drumettes with Sweet Potato Wedges

Prep Time: 20 Minutes   Cook Time: 45 Minutes   Serves: 4-6

Ingredients:

- 2 lbs chicken drumettes
- 1/2 cup barbecue sauce
- 2 tablespoons olive oil
- 1 teaspoon smoked paprika
- Salt and pepper to taste
- 4 medium sweet potatoes, cut into wedges

Directions:

1. Preheat one side of your Ninja Foodi 2-Basket Air Fryer to Bake at 375°F.
2. In a bowl, toss chicken drumettes with barbecue sauce, olive oil, smoked paprika, salt, and pepper.
3. Place the coated drumettes in one basket.
4. Bake for 30-35 minutes, turning halfway through, or until the chicken reaches an internal temperature of 175°F.
5. At the same time, preheat the other side of the Air Fryer to Air Fry at 400°F.
6. Toss sweet potato wedges with olive oil, salt, and pepper.
7. Place the seasoned sweet potatoes in the second basket and air fry for 15-20 minutes, shaking the basket halfway through.
8. Press the Smart Finish button.
9. Serve the BBQ chicken drumettes with a side of crispy sweet potato wedges.

Nutritional Value (Amount per Serving):

Calories: 395; Fat: 10.73; Carb: 34.17; Protein: 39.02

Lemon Herb Air-Roasted Cornish Hens with Quinoa Salad

Prep Time: 25 Minutes   Cook Time: 1 Hour   Serves: 4

Ingredients:

- 4 Cornish hens
- 1/4 cup olive oil
- Zest and juice of 2 lemons
- 2 teaspoons dried thyme
- 1 teaspoon dried rosemary
- Salt and pepper to taste
- 2 cups cooked quinoa
- 1 cucumber, diced
- 1 cup cherry tomatoes, halved
- 1/4 cup fresh parsley, chopped

Directions:

1. Preheat one side of your Ninja Foodi 2-Basket Air Fryer to Roast at 375°F.

2. In a bowl, mix olive oil, lemon zest, lemon juice, dried thyme, dried rosemary, salt, and pepper.
3. Rub each Cornish hen with the lemon herb mixture and place them in one basket.
4. Roast for 50-55 minutes, turning halfway through, or until the internal temperature reaches 165°F.
5. In a separate bowl, combine cooked quinoa, diced cucumber, cherry tomatoes, and chopped fresh parsley to make the quinoa salad.
6. Serve the lemon herb air-roasted Cornish hens with a refreshing quinoa salad.

Nutritional Value (Amount per Serving):

Calories: 1409; Fat: 48.79; Carb: 24.21; Protein: 205.24

Buffalo-Spiced Chicken Tenders with Blue Cheese Dip

Prep Time: 15 Minutes   Cook Time: 20 Minutes   Serves: 4-6

Ingredients:

- 2 lbs chicken tenders
- 1/2 cup buffalo sauce
- 2 tablespoons melted butter
- 1 teaspoon garlic powder
- Salt and pepper to taste
- Blue cheese dressing for dipping

Directions:

1. Preheat one side of your Ninja Foodi 2-Basket Air Fryer to Air Fry at 375°F.
2. In a bowl, mix buffalo sauce, melted butter, garlic powder, salt, and pepper.
3. Toss chicken tenders in the buffalo sauce mixture and place them in one basket.
4. Air fry for 15-20 minutes, turning halfway through, or until the chicken is cooked through.
5. Serve the buffalo-spiced chicken tenders with blue cheese dressing for dipping.

Nutritional Value (Amount per Serving):

Calories: 580; Fat: 31.1; Carb: 45.1; Protein: 30.31

Teriyaki-Glazed Air-Baked Chicken Wings with Broccoli Slaw

Prep Time: 20 Minutes   Cook Time: 35 Minutes   Serves: 4-6

Ingredients:

- 2 lbs chicken wings, split at joints
- 1/2 cup teriyaki sauce

- 2 tablespoons soy sauce
- 1 tablespoon honey
- 1 teaspoon sesame oil
- 1 teaspoon garlic powder
- Salt and pepper to taste
- 4 cups broccoli slaw mix

Directions:

1. Preheat one side of your Ninja Foodi 2-Basket Air Fryer to Bake at 375°F.
2. In a bowl, combine teriyaki sauce, soy sauce, honey, sesame oil, garlic powder, salt, and pepper.
3. Toss chicken wings in the teriyaki mixture and place them in one basket.
4. Bake for 25-30 minutes, turning halfway through, or until the wings are crispy.
5. Toss broccoli slaw mix with a bit of teriyaki sauce mixture.
6. Serve teriyaki-glazed chicken wings with a side of refreshing broccoli slaw.

Nutritional Value (Amount per Serving):

Calories: 472; Fat: 20.2; Carb: 27.05; Protein: 45.5

Cilantro-Lime Air-Dehydrated Turkey Jerky with Pineapple Salsa

Prep Time: 15 Minutes   Cook Time: 4-6 Hours   Serves: 4

Ingredients:

- 1.5 lbs turkey breast, thinly sliced
- 1/2 cup fresh cilantro, chopped
- Zest and juice of 2 limes
- 1 teaspoon cumin
- 1/2 teaspoon chili powder
- Salt and pepper to taste
- 1 cup diced pineapple
- 1/4 cup red onion, finely chopped

Directions:

1. In a bowl, combine turkey slices with chopped cilantro, lime zest, lime juice, cumin, chili powder, salt, and pepper. Marinate in the refrigerator for at least 2 hours or overnight.
2. Preheat one side of your Ninja Foodi 2-Basket Air Fryer to Dehydrate at 160°F.
3. Press the Smart Finish button.
4. Arrange marinated turkey slices in air fryer basket, ensuring they are not touching.
5. Dehydrate for 4-6 hours or until the turkey becomes jerky-like, flipping the slices halfway through.

6. In a separate bowl, combine diced pineapple and finely chopped red onion to make the pineapple salsa.
7. Serve the cilantro-lime turkey jerky with a side of vibrant pineapple salsa.

Nutritional Value (Amount per Serving):

Calories: 321; Fat: 12.21; Carb: 13.84; Protein: 38.08

Herbed Lemon Chicken Thighs with Garlic Parmesan Broccoli

Prep Time: 20 Minutes   Cook Time: 45 Minutes   Serves: 4-6

Ingredients:

- 2 lbs chicken thighs, bone-in, skin-on
- 3 tablespoons olive oil
- Zest and juice of 1 lemon
- 2 teaspoons dried thyme
- 1 teaspoon dried rosemary
- Salt and pepper to taste
- 1 lb broccoli florets
- 3 cloves garlic, minced
- 1/4 cup grated Parmesan cheese

Directions:

1. Preheat one side of your Ninja Foodi 2-Basket Air Fryer to Roast at 375°F.
2. In a bowl, mix olive oil, lemon zest, lemon juice, dried thyme, dried rosemary, salt, and pepper.
3. Coat chicken thighs with the herbed lemon mixture and place them in one basket.
4. Roast for 35-40 minutes, turning halfway through, or until the chicken reaches an internal temperature of 175°F.
5. At the same time, preheat the other side of the Air Fryer to Air Fry at 400°F.
6. Toss broccoli with olive oil, minced garlic, salt, and pepper.
7. Place the seasoned broccoli in the second basket and air fry for 10-15 minutes.
8. Press the Smart Finish button.
9. Sprinkle grated Parmesan cheese over the broccoli and serve alongside the herbed lemon chicken thighs.

Nutritional Value (Amount per Serving):

Calories: 522; Fat: 40.14; Carb: 5.95; Protein: 34.62

Orange Glazed Chicken Wings with Asian Cabbage Slaw

Prep Time: 20 Minutes   Cook Time: 35 Minutes   Serves: 4-6

Ingredients:

- 2 lbs chicken wings, split at joints
- 1/2 cup orange marmalade
- 2 tablespoons soy sauce
- 1 tablespoon rice vinegar
- 1 teaspoon grated ginger
- Salt and pepper to taste
- 4 cups shredded Napa cabbage
- 1 carrot, julienned
- 2 green onions, sliced
- Sesame seeds for garnish

Directions:

1. Preheat one side of your Ninja Foodi 2-Basket Air Fryer to Bake at 375°F.
2. In a bowl, mix orange marmalade, soy sauce, rice vinegar, grated ginger, salt, and pepper.
3. Toss chicken wings in the orange glaze and place them in one basket.
4. Bake for 25-30 minutes, turning halfway through, or until the wings are crispy.
5. In a separate bowl, combine shredded Napa cabbage, julienned carrot, and sliced green onions to make the Asian cabbage slaw.
6. Serve the orange-glazed chicken wings with a side of refreshing Asian cabbage slaw, garnished with sesame seeds.

Nutritional Value (Amount per Serving):

Calories: 365; Fat: 8.37; Carb: 30.18; Protein: 42.33

Chapter 3: Beef, Pork and Lamb

Cajun-Spiced Beef Skewers with Corn on the Cob

Prep Time: 20 Minutes   Cook Time: 25 Minutes   Serves: 4

Ingredients:

- 1.5 pounds beef sirloin, cut into cubes
- 3 tablespoons olive oil
- 2 tablespoons Cajun seasoning
- 1 teaspoon smoked paprika
- 1 teaspoon onion powder
- Salt and pepper to taste
- 4 ears of corn, husked and halved

Directions:

1. Preheat one side of your Air Fryer to Air Broil at 400°F.
2. In a bowl, mix olive oil, Cajun seasoning, smoked paprika, onion powder, salt, and pepper.
3. Thread beef cubes onto skewers and brush them with the Cajun spice mixture. Place them in one basket.
4. Air broil the beef skewers for 20-25 minutes, turning occasionally, or until they are cooked to your desired doneness.
5. At the same time, preheat the other side of the Air Fryer to Roast at 375°F.
6. Place corn on the cob in the second basket and roast for 15-20 minutes or until the kernels are tender.
7. Press the Smart Finish button.
8. Serve the Cajun-spiced beef skewers with a side of roasted corn.

Nutritional Value (Amount per Serving):

Calories: 556; Fat: 30.85; Carb: 31.53; Protein: 40.34

Honey-Garlic Glazed Pork Belly Bites with Pineapple Salsa

Prep Time: 15 Minutes   Cook Time: 40 Minutes   Serves: 4

Ingredients:

- 1.5 pounds pork belly, cut into bite-sized pieces
- 1/4 cup honey
- 3 tablespoons soy sauce
- 2 tablespoons rice vinegar
- 2 cloves garlic, minced
- 1 teaspoon grated fresh ginger
- Salt and pepper to taste

- 1 cup pineapple, diced

Directions:

1. Preheat one side of your Air Fryer to Air Fry at 375°F.
2. In a bowl, whisk together honey, soy sauce, rice vinegar, minced garlic, grated ginger, salt, and pepper.
3. Toss pork belly pieces in the honey-garlic mixture and place them in one basket.
4. Air fry the pork belly bites for 35-40 minutes, turning halfway through, or until they are crispy and golden brown.
5. At the same time, preheat the other side of the Air Fryer to Roast at 400°F.
6. In a separate bowl, mix diced pineapple with a pinch of salt.
7. Roast the pineapple in the second basket for 10-15 minutes or until it caramelizes slightly.
8. Press the Smart Finish button.
9. Serve the honey-garlic glazed pork belly bites with a refreshing pineapple salsa.

Nutritional Value (Amount per Serving):

Calories: 1026; Fat: 92.42; Carb: 31.93; Protein: 17.39

Mediterranean Lamb Kebabs with Greek Salad

Prep Time: 25 Minutes   Cook Time: 30 Minutes   Serves: 4

Ingredients:

- 1.5 pounds lamb leg meat, cut into chunks
- 3 tablespoons olive oil
- 2 teaspoons dried oregano
- 1 teaspoon ground cumin
- 1 teaspoon minced garlic
- Kalamata olives for garnish
- Salt and pepper to taste
- 2 cucumbers, diced
- 2 tomatoes, diced
- 1 red onion, finely chopped
- 1/2 cup feta cheese, crumbled

Directions:

1. Preheat one side of your Air Fryer to Roast at 375°F.
2. In a bowl, combine olive oil, dried oregano, ground cumin, minced garlic, salt, and pepper.
3. Thread lamb chunks onto skewers and brush them with the Mediterranean spice mixture. Place them in one basket.
4. Roast the lamb kebabs for 25-30 minutes, turning occasionally, or until they are cooked to your desired doneness.
5. At the same time, preheat the other side of the Air Fryer to Dehydrate at 130°F.

6. In a large bowl, mix diced cucumbers, tomatoes, red onion, and crumbled feta to make the Greek salad.
7. Dehydrate the Greek salad for 20-25 minutes, stirring occasionally, to intensify flavors.
8. Press the Smart Finish button.
9. Serve the Mediterranean lamb kebabs over a bed of dehydrated Greek salad and garnish with Kalamata olives.

Nutritional Value (Amount per Serving):

Calories: 419; Fat: 23.24; Carb: 12.67; Protein: 39.16

Smoky Pulled Pork Sliders with Coleslaw

Prep Time: 20 Minutes   Cook Time: 4 Hours   Serves: 4

Ingredients:

- 2 pounds pork shoulder, trimmed and cut into chunks
- 1 cup barbecue sauce
- 2 tablespoons apple cider vinegar
- 1 tablespoon smoked paprika
- 1 teaspoon onion powder
- 1 teaspoon garlic powder
- Salt and pepper to taste
- 8 slider buns
- Coleslaw for topping

Directions:

1. In a bowl, mix barbecue sauce, apple cider vinegar, smoked paprika, onion powder, garlic powder, salt, and pepper.
2. Marinate the pork chunks in the barbecue mixture for at least 2 hours, preferably overnight.
3. Preheat one side of your Air Fryer to Roast at 375°F.
4. Transfer the marinated pork to one basket and roast for 3-4 hours until it's fork-tender and can be easily pulled apart.
5. At the same time, preheat the other side of the Air Fryer to Bake at 350°F.
6. Bake the slider buns in the second basket for 5-7 minutes or until they are golden brown.
7. Press the Smart Finish button.
8. Shred the roasted pork and assemble the sliders with a generous topping of coleslaw.
9. Serve the smoky pulled pork sliders with your favorite side.

Nutritional Value (Amount per Serving):

Calories: 1335; Fat: 75.48; Carb: 96.32; Protein: 63.91

Herb-Marinated Beef Tenderloin with Roasted Vegetables

Prep Time: 30 Minutes   Cook Time: 40 Minutes   Serves: 4

Ingredients:

- 2 beef tenderloin steaks (about 8 ounces each)
- 4 tablespoons balsamic vinegar
- 3 tablespoons olive oil
- 2 teaspoons dried thyme
- 1 teaspoon dried rosemary
- 1 teaspoon minced garlic
- Salt and pepper to taste
- 1 cup baby potatoes, halved
- 1 cup baby carrots
- 1 cup cherry tomatoes

Directions:

1. Preheat one side of your Air Fryer to Air Broil at 400°F.
2. In a bowl, mix balsamic vinegar, olive oil, dried thyme, dried rosemary, minced garlic, salt, and pepper.
3. Marinate the beef tenderloin steaks in the herb mixture for 20-30 minutes.
4. Place the marinated beef in one basket and air broil for 15-20 minutes, turning halfway through, or until the steaks reach your preferred level of doneness.
5. At the same time, preheat the other side of the Air Fryer to Roast at 375°F.
6. Toss baby potatoes, baby carrots, and cherry tomatoes with olive oil, salt, and pepper.
7. Roast the vegetables in the second basket for 20-25 minutes or until they are tender and golden.
8. Press the Smart Finish button.
9. Serve the herb-marinated beef tenderloin steaks with a side of roasted vegetables.

Nutritional Value (Amount per Serving):

Calories: 285; Fat: 15.48; Carb: 16.37; Protein: 19.46

Maple-Dijon Glazed Pork Loin with Maple-Roasted Brussels Sprouts

Prep Time: 20 Minutes   Cook Time: 35 Minutes   Serves: 4

Ingredients:

- 1.5 pounds pork loin, trimmed
- 1/4 cup maple syrup
- 2 tablespoons Dijon mustard
- 2 tablespoons olive oil
- 1 teaspoon dried thyme
- Salt and pepper to taste
- 4 cups Brussels sprouts, halved

Directions:

1. Preheat one side of your Air Fryer to Roast at 375°F.
2. In a bowl, whisk together maple syrup, Dijon mustard, olive oil, dried thyme, salt, and pepper.
3. Brush the pork loin with the maple-Dijon glaze and place it in one basket.
4. Air roast the pork loin for 30-35 minutes, turning halfway through, or until the internal temperature reaches 145°F.
5. At the same time, preheat the other side of the Air Fryer to Roast at 400°F.
6. Toss Brussels sprouts with a bit of olive oil, salt, and pepper.
7. Roast the Brussels sprouts in the second basket for 15-20 minutes or until they are crispy and golden.
8. Press the Match Cook button.
9. Serve the maple-Dijon glazed pork loin with a side of maple-roasted Brussels sprouts.

Nutritional Value (Amount per Serving):

Calories: 514; Fat: 26.12; Carb: 22.65; Protein: 47.07

Herb-Crusted Lamb Chops with Garlic Mashed Potatoes

Prep Time: 25 Minutes   Cook Time: 25 Minutes   Serves: 4

Ingredients:

- 8 lamb chops
- 3 tablespoons olive oil
- 2 teaspoons dried rosemary
- 1 teaspoon dried thyme
- 1 teaspoon minced garlic
- Salt and pepper to taste
- 4 cups potatoes, peeled and diced
- 1/2 cup milk
- 4 tablespoons butter

Directions:

1. Preheat one side of your Air Fryer to Air Fry at 375°F.
2. In a bowl, combine olive oil, dried rosemary, dried thyme, minced garlic, salt, and pepper.
3. Coat each lamb chop with the herb mixture and place them in one basket.
4. Air fry the lamb chops for 20-25 minutes, turning halfway through, or until they reach the desired level of doneness.
5. At the same time, preheat the other side of the Air Fryer to Air Broil at 400°F.
6. Boil potatoes until tender, then mash them with milk, butter, salt, and pepper.
7. Broil the mashed potatoes in the second basket for 5-7 minutes, or until

they develop a golden crust.

8. Press the Smart Finish button.
9. Serve the herb-crusted lamb chops over a bed of garlic mashed potatoes.

Nutritional Value (Amount per Serving):

Calories: 1137; Fat: 61.83; Carb: 29.09; Protein: 117.69

Lemon-Herb Chicken Thighs with Baked Sweet Potatoes

Prep Time: 20 Minutes   Cook Time: 35 Minutes   Serves: 4

Ingredients:

- 8 bone-in, skin-on chicken thighs
- Zest and juice of 2 lemons
- 3 tablespoons olive oil
- 2 teaspoons dried oregano
- 1 teaspoon smoked paprika
- Salt and pepper to taste
- 4 medium-sized sweet potatoes, cubed

Directions:

1. Preheat one side of your Air Fryer to Roast at 400°F.
2. In a bowl, combine lemon zest, lemon juice, olive oil, dried oregano, smoked paprika, salt, and pepper.
3. Rub each chicken thigh with the lemon-herb mixture and place them in one basket.
4. Roast the chicken thighs for 30-35 minutes, turning halfway through, or until the internal temperature reaches 165°F.
5. At the same time, preheat the other side of the Air Fryer to Bake at 375°F.
6. Toss sweet potato cubes with olive oil, salt, and pepper.
7. Place the seasoned sweet potatoes in the second basket and bake for 20-25 minutes, or until they are tender and lightly browned.
8. Press the Smart Finish button.
9. Serve the lemon-herb chicken thighs over a bed of baked sweet potatoes.

Nutritional Value (Amount per Serving):

Calories: 1317; Fat: 121.09; Carb: 32.11; Protein: 26.45

Korean BBQ Beef Bulgogi with Stir-Fried Vegetables

Prep Time: 30 Minutes   Cook Time: 25 Minutes   Serves: 4

Ingredients:

- 1.5 pounds beef sirloin, thinly sliced
- 1/2 cup soy sauce
- 1/4 cup brown sugar
- 2 tablespoons sesame oil
- 2 tablespoons rice vinegar
- 2 cloves garlic, minced
- 1 teaspoon grated ginger
- 1 cup broccoli florets
- 1 cup bell peppers, sliced
- 1 cup snow peas, trimmed

Directions:

1. In a bowl, mix soy sauce, brown sugar, sesame oil, rice vinegar, minced garlic, and grated ginger.
2. Marinate the sliced beef in the Korean BBQ mixture for at least 20-30 minutes.
3. Preheat one side of your Air Fryer to Air Fry at 400°F.
4. Air fry the marinated beef in one basket for 10-15 minutes or until it's cooked through.
5. At the same time, preheat the other side of the Air Fryer to Roast at 375°F.
6. Roast the stir-fried vegetables in the second basket for 10-12 minutes.
7. Press the Smart Finish button.
8. Serve the Korean BBQ beef bulgogi over a bed of stir-fried vegetables.

Nutritional Value (Amount per Serving):

Calories: 538; Fat: 31.58; Carb: 23.48; Protein: 38.14

Tuscan Pork Tenderloin with Roasted Root Vegetables

Prep Time: 20 Minutes   Cook Time: 40 Minutes   Serves: 4

Ingredients:

- 2 pork tenderloins (about 1 pound each)
- 1/4 cup balsamic vinegar
- 3 tablespoons olive oil
- 2 teaspoons dried Italian seasoning
- 1 teaspoon garlic powder
- Salt and pepper to taste
- 4 cups mixed root vegetables (carrots, parsnips, sweet potatoes), peeled and diced

Directions:

1. Preheat one side of your Air Fryer to Roast at 375°F.
2. In a bowl, combine balsamic vinegar, olive oil, dried Italian seasoning, garlic powder, salt, and pepper.
3. Coat each pork tenderloin with the Tuscan mixture and place them in one

basket.

4. Roast the pork tenderloins for 35-40 minutes, turning halfway through, or until the internal temperature reaches 145°F.
5. At the same time, preheat the other side of the Air Fryer to Roast at 400°F.
6. Toss mixed root vegetables with a bit of olive oil, salt, and pepper.
7. Roast the root vegetables in the second basket for 20-25 minutes or until they are tender and caramelized.
8. Press the Match Cook button.
9. Serve the Tuscan pork tenderloin with a side of roasted root vegetables.

Nutritional Value (Amount per Serving):

Calories: 507; Fat: 18.55; Carb: 18.5; Protein: 62.51

Garlic-Herb Beef Striploin with Grilled Asparagus

Prep Time: 25 Minutes   Cook Time: 30 Minutes   Serves: 4

Ingredients:

- 4 beef striploin steaks (about 1 inch thick)
- 4 tablespoons olive oil
- 2 teaspoons dried thyme
- 1 teaspoon dried rosemary
- 1 teaspoon minced garlic
- Salt and pepper to taste
- 1 bunch asparagus, trimmed
- Lemon wedges for serving

Directions:

1. Preheat one side of your Air Fryer to Air Broil at 400°F.
2. In a bowl, mix olive oil, dried thyme, dried rosemary, minced garlic, salt, and pepper.
3. Rub each beef striploin with the garlic-herb mixture and place them in one basket.
4. Air broil the beef striploins for 25-30 minutes, turning halfway through, or until they reach the desired level of doneness.
5. At the same time, preheat the other side of the Air Fryer to Roast at 375°F.
6. Roast the asparagus in the second basket for 10-15 minutes, turning occasionally, until they are tender and lightly charred.
7. Press the Smart Finish button.
8. Serve the garlic-herb beef striploin steaks with a side of grilled asparagus and lemon wedges.

Nutritional Value (Amount per Serving):

Calories: 506; Fat: 41.12; Carb: 3.63; Protein: 29.98

Asian-Inspired Beef and Broccoli

Prep Time: 20 Minutes   Cook Time: 15 Minutes   Serves: 4

Ingredients:

- 1.5 pounds flank steak, thinly sliced
- 1/2 cup soy sauce
- 3 tablespoons oyster sauce
- 2 tablespoons hoisin sauce
- 1 tablespoon sesame oil
- 1 tablespoon cornstarch
- 2 tablespoons vegetable oil
- 4 cups broccoli florets
- 1 cup sliced bell peppers (any color)
- 2 green onions, sliced (for garnish)
- Cooked white rice for serving

Directions:

1. In a bowl, mix soy sauce, oyster sauce, hoisin sauce, sesame oil, and cornstarch.
2. Marinate the sliced flank steak in the Asian-inspired sauce for 15-20 minutes.
3. Preheat one side of your Air Fryer to Air Fry at 400°F.
4. Air fry the marinated beef in one basket for 8-10 minutes or until it's cooked through.
5. At the same time, preheat the other side of the Air Fryer to Roast at 375°F.
6. Roast the stir-fried vegetables in the second basket for 5-7 minutes.
7. Press the Smart Finish button.
8. Serve the Asian-inspired beef and broccoli over cooked white rice, garnished with sliced green onions.

Nutritional Value (Amount per Serving):

Calories: 482; Fat: 25.4; Carb: 21.71; Protein: 41.38

Stuffed Pork Tenderloin with Apple-Walnut Filling

Prep Time: 30 Minutes   Cook Time: 35 Minutes   Serves: 4

Ingredients:

- 2 pork tenderloins (about 1 pound each)
- 1 cup diced apples
- 1/2 cup chopped walnuts
- 2 tablespoons maple syrup
- 1 teaspoon ground cinnamon
- Salt and pepper to taste
- 2 tablespoons Dijon mustard
- 2 tablespoons olive oil

Directions:

1. Preheat one side of your Air Fryer to Roast at 375°F.

2. In a bowl, combine diced apples, chopped walnuts, maple syrup, ground cinnamon, salt, and pepper.
3. Butterfly each pork tenderloin and fill with the apple-walnut mixture. Secure with kitchen twine.
4. Brush the stuffed pork tenderloins with Dijon mustard and olive oil, then place them in one basket.
5. Roast the stuffed pork tenderloins for 30-35 minutes, turning halfway through, or until the internal temperature reaches 145°F.
6. At the same time, preheat the other side of the Air Fryer to Bake at 400°F.
7. Bake any remaining apple-walnut filling in the second basket for 15-20 minutes, or until it's caramelized.
8. Press the Smart Finish button.
9. Serve the stuffed pork tenderloin slices with the baked apple-walnut filling on the side.

Nutritional Value (Amount per Serving):

Calories: 500; Fat: 21.57; Carb: 13.88; Protein: 61.49

Herb-Infused Lamb Shoulder Chops with Mint Yogurt Sauce

Prep Time: 25 Minutes   Cook Time: 30 Minutes   Serves: 4

Ingredients:

- 4 lamb shoulder chops
- 3 tablespoons olive oil
- 2 teaspoons dried mint
- 1 teaspoon dried rosemary
- 1 teaspoon minced garlic
- Salt and pepper to taste
- 1 cup plain Greek yogurt
- 2 tablespoons fresh mint, chopped
- Lemon wedges for serving

Directions:

1. Preheat one side of your Air Fryer to Air Broil at 400°F.
2. In a bowl, mix olive oil, dried mint, dried rosemary, minced garlic, salt, and pepper.
3. Brush each lamb shoulder chop with the herb-infused mixture and place them in one basket.
4. Air broil the lamb chops for 25-30 minutes, turning halfway through, or until they reach the desired level of doneness.
5. At the same time, preheat the other side of the Air Fryer to Dehydrate at 130°F.
6. In a separate bowl, mix Greek yogurt with fresh chopped mint.
7. Dehydrate the mint yogurt sauce in the second basket for 15-20 minutes, stirring occasionally, to intensify flavors.

8. Press the Smart Finish button.
9. Serve the herb-infused lamb shoulder chops with a dollop of mint yogurt sauce and lemon wedges.

Nutritional Value (Amount per Serving):

Calories: 1040; Fat: 60.3; Carb: 4.33; Protein: 119.78

Coffee-Rubbed Beef Tri-Tip with Roasted Zucchini

Prep Time: 15 Minutes   Cook Time: 40 Minutes   Serves: 4

Ingredients:

- 2 pounds beef tri-tip roast
- 2 tablespoons ground coffee
- 1 tablespoon brown sugar
- 1 teaspoon smoked paprika
- 1 teaspoon garlic powder
- Salt and pepper to taste
- 4 medium zucchinis, sliced
- Olive oil for brushing

Directions:

1. Preheat one side of your Air Fryer to Roast at 375°F.
2. In a bowl, mix ground coffee, brown sugar, smoked paprika, garlic powder, salt, and pepper.
3. Rub the coffee mixture onto the beef tri-tip and place it in one basket.
4. Roast the beef tri-tip for 35-40 minutes, turning halfway through, or until it reaches the desired level of doneness.
5. At the same time, preheat the other side of the Air Fryer to Roast at 400°F.
6. Brush zucchini slices with olive oil, sprinkle with salt and pepper.
7. Roast the zucchini in the second basket for 10-15 minutes or until they are tender and have grill marks.
8. Press the Smart Finish button.
9. Serve the coffee-rubbed beef tri-tip slices with roasted zucchini on the side.

Nutritional Value (Amount per Serving):

Calories: 533; Fat: 29.43; Carb: 3.07; Protein: 60.71

Balsamic-Glazed Lamb Shanks with Roasted Garlic Mashed Potatoes

Prep Time: 30 Minutes   Cook Time: 3 Hours   Serves: 4

Ingredients:

- 4 lamb shanks
- 1 cup balsamic vinegar
- 3 tablespoons olive oil
- 2 tablespoons honey
- 1 teaspoon dried rosemary
- 1 teaspoon minced garlic

- Salt and pepper to taste
- 4 cups potatoes, peeled and diced
- 1/2 cup milk
- 4 tablespoons butter
- Roasted garlic cloves (from 1 bulb)

Directions:

1. Preheat one side of your Air Fryer to Roast at 375°F.
2. In a bowl, combine balsamic vinegar, olive oil, honey, dried rosemary, minced garlic, salt, and pepper.
3. Place lamb shanks in a baking dish, pour the balsamic glaze over them, and roast in one basket for 2.5-3 hours or until lamb is tender.
4. While the lamb is cooking, preheat the other side of the Air Fryer to Bake at 400°F.
5. Boil potatoes until tender, then mash them with milk, butter, and roasted garlic cloves.
6. Bake the roasted garlic mashed potatoes in the second basket for 15-20 minutes, or until they develop a golden crust.
7. Press the Smart Finish button.
8. Serve the balsamic-glazed lamb shanks over a bed of roasted garlic mashed potatoes.

Nutritional Value (Amount per Serving):

Calories: 974; Fat: 39.92; Carb: 48.76; Protein: 104.8

Chapter 4: Fish and Seafood

Coconut-Crusted Shrimp with Mango Salsa

Prep Time: 20 Minutes   Cook Time: 15 Minutes   Serves: 4

Ingredients:

- 1 pound large shrimp, peeled and deveined
- 1 cup shredded coconut
- 1 cup panko breadcrumbs
- 2 eggs, beaten
- Salt and pepper to taste
- 2 mangoes, diced
- 1 red bell pepper, finely chopped
- 1/4 cup chopped fresh cilantro
- 1 tablespoon lime juice

Directions:

1. Preheat one side of your Air Fryer to Air Fry at 375°F.
2. In one bowl, mix shredded coconut and panko breadcrumbs. In another bowl, beat the eggs.
3. Dip each shrimp into the beaten eggs, then coat them with the coconut-breadcrumb mixture. Place in one basket.
4. Air fry the shrimp for 12-15 minutes until golden brown and crispy, turning once.
5. At the same time, preheat the other side of the Air Fryer to Dehydrate at 130°F.
6. In a bowl, combine diced mangoes, chopped red bell pepper, cilantro, and lime juice to make the salsa.
7. Dehydrate the mango salsa for 30-40 minutes, or until it reaches a slightly dried consistency.
8. Press the Smart Finish button.
9. Serve the coconut-crusted shrimp with mango salsa on the side.

Nutritional Value (Amount per Serving):

Calories: 149; Fat: 5.49; Carb: 20.02; Protein: 6.75

Herb-Grilled Swordfish with Lemon-Basil Quinoa

Prep Time: 15 Minutes   Cook Time: 20 Minutes   Serves: 4

Ingredients:

- 4 swordfish steaks
- 3 tablespoons olive oil
- 2 tablespoons chopped fresh herbs (rosemary, thyme, and parsley)

- Zest and juice of 1 lemon
- Salt and pepper to taste
- 1 cup quinoa, cooked
- 1/4 cup chopped fresh basil

Directions:

1. Preheat one side of your Air Fryer to Air Broil at 400°F.
2. Brush swordfish steaks with olive oil and sprinkle with chopped herbs, lemon zest, salt, and pepper. Place them in one basket.
3. Air broil the swordfish for 18-20 minutes, turning once, until it's grill-marked and cooked through.
4. At the same time, preheat the other side of the Air Fryer to Bake at 375°F.
5. Fluff the cooked quinoa with a fork and mix in chopped fresh basil.
6. Bake the lemon-basil quinoa for 10-15 minutes until it's warmed through.
7. Press the Smart Finish button.
8. Serve the herb-grilled swordfish over a bed of lemon-basil quinoa.

Nutritional Value (Amount per Serving):

Calories: 749; Fat: 45.51; Carb: 29.49; Protein: 52.76

Blackened Red Snapper Tacos with Avocado Crema

Prep Time: 20 Minutes   Cook Time: 15 Minutes   Serves: 4

Ingredients:

- 4 red snapper fillets
- 2 tablespoons blackened seasoning
- 1 cup shredded cabbage
- 1/2 cup diced tomatoes
- 1/4 cup chopped red onion
- 1/4 cup chopped fresh cilantro
- 8 small corn tortillas
- 1 ripe avocado
- 1/4 cup sour cream
- Juice of 1 lime
- Salt and pepper to taste

Directions:

1. Preheat one side of your Air Fryer to Air Fry at 375°F.
2. Rub red snapper fillets with blackened seasoning, salt, and pepper. Place them in one basket.
3. Air fry the red snapper for 12-15 minutes until it's blackened and flakes easily.
4. At the same time, preheat the other side of the Air Fryer to Air Broil at 400°F.
5. Air broil corn tortillas for 2-3 minutes until they're warm and slightly crispy.
6. Press the Smart Finish button.
7. In a bowl, mix shredded cabbage, diced tomatoes, chopped red onion, and

cilantro to make the taco slaw. Set aside.

8. In a blender, blend avocado, sour cream, lime juice, salt, and pepper to make the avocado crema.

9. Assemble tacos with blackened red snapper, taco slaw, and drizzle with avocado crema.

Nutritional Value (Amount per Serving):

Calories: 291; Fat: 10.44; Carb: 47.52; Protein: 5.76

Mediterranean Grilled Octopus Salad

Prep Time: 25 Minutes   Cook Time: 20 Minutes   Serves: 4

Ingredients:

- 2 pounds octopus, cleaned
- 3 tablespoons olive oil
- 2 cloves garlic, minced
- 1 teaspoon dried oregano
- Zest and juice of 1 lemon
- Salt and pepper to taste
- 2 cups mixed greens
- 1 cup cherry tomatoes, halved
- 1/2 cup Kalamata olives, pitted and sliced
- 1/4 cup crumbled feta cheese

Directions:

1. Preheat one side of your Air Fryer to Roast at 400°F.

2. In a bowl, mix olive oil, minced garlic, dried oregano, lemon zest, lemon juice, salt, and pepper.

3. Marinate cleaned octopus in the mixture and place it in one basket.

4. Roast the octopus for 18-20 minutes, turning once, until it's tender and slightly charred.

5. In a large bowl, combine mixed greens, cherry tomatoes, Kalamata olives, and crumbled feta cheese.

6. Serve the Mediterranean grilled octopus over the warm salad.

Nutritional Value (Amount per Serving):

Calories: 335; Fat: 16.37; Carb: 10.14; Protein: 36.11

Sesame-Ginger Glazed Tuna Steaks with Stir-Fried Vegetables

Prep Time: 15 Minutes   Cook Time: 15 Minutes   Serves: 4

Ingredients:

- 4 tuna steaks
- 1/4 cup soy sauce
- 2 tablespoons sesame oil
- 1 tablespoon grated ginger

- 2 cloves garlic, minced
- 2 tablespoons honey
- 1 cup broccoli florets
- 1 cup snap peas, trimmed
- 1 red bell pepper, sliced
- 2 tablespoons vegetable oil
- Sesame seeds for garnish

Directions:

1. Preheat one side of your Air Fryer to Air Broil at 400°F.
2. In a bowl, mix soy sauce, sesame oil, grated ginger, minced garlic, and honey.
3. Brush tuna steaks with the sesame-ginger glaze and place them in one basket.
4. Air broil the tuna for 12-15 minutes until it's seared and cooked to your liking.
5. At the same time, preheat the other side of the Air Fryer to Air Fry at 375°F.
6. Air fry broccoli, snap peas, and red bell pepper in vegetable oil until crisp-tender.
7. Press the Smart Finish button.
8. Serve sesame-ginger glazed tuna steaks over a bed of stir-fried vegetables, garnished with sesame seeds.

Nutritional Value (Amount per Serving):

Calories: 706; Fat: 49.72; Carb: 14.87; Protein: 48.37

Pesto-Grilled Halibut with Roasted Cherry Tomatoes

Prep Time: 15 Minutes   Cook Time: 18 Minutes   Serves: 4

Ingredients:

- 4 halibut fillets
- 1/2 cup pesto sauce
- Zest and juice of 1 lemon
- Salt and pepper to taste
- 1 pint cherry tomatoes, halved
- 2 tablespoons olive oil
- 1 tablespoon balsamic glaze

Directions:

1. Preheat one side of your Air Fryer to Air Broil at 400°F.
2. Brush halibut fillets with pesto sauce and sprinkle with lemon zest, lemon juice, salt, and pepper. Place them in one basket.
3. Air broil the halibut for 15-18 minutes until it's cooked through and slightly browned.
4. At the same time, preheat the other side of the Air Fryer to Roast at 375°F.
5. Toss halved cherry tomatoes with olive oil, salt, and pepper.
6. Roast the cherry tomatoes for 8-10 minutes until they are caramelized.
7. Press the Smart Finish button.
8. Drizzle the roasted cherry tomatoes with balsamic glaze and serve over the pesto-grilled halibut.

Nutritional Value (Amount per Serving):

Calories: 998; Fat: 80.34; Carb: 4.61; Protein: 62.25

Honey-Lime Glazed Tilapia with Cilantro-Lime Rice

Prep Time: 15 Minutes   Cook Time: 20 Minutes   Serves: 4

Ingredients:

- 4 tilapia fillets
- 1/4 cup honey
- Zest and juice of 2 limes
- 2 tablespoons soy sauce
- 2 teaspoons minced garlic
- 1 cup white rice, cooked
- 1/4 cup chopped fresh cilantro
- Lime wedges for serving

Directions:

1. Preheat one side of your Air Fryer to Roast at 400°F.
2. In a bowl, whisk together honey, lime zest, lime juice, soy sauce, and minced garlic.
3. Brush tilapia fillets with the honey-lime glaze and place them in one basket.
4. Roast the tilapia for 18-20 minutes until it's glazed and flakes easily.
5. At the same time, preheat the other side of the Air Fryer to Bake at 375°F.
6. Mix cooked white rice with chopped cilantro and bake for 10-12 minutes until it's heated through.
7. Press the Smart Finish button.
8. Serve the honey-lime glazed tilapia over a bed of cilantro-lime rice, accompanied by lime wedges.

Nutritional Value (Amount per Serving):

Calories: 381; Fat: 3.7; Carb: 60.51; Protein: 27.32

Lemon-Dill Grilled Scallops with Orzo Salad

Prep Time: 20 Minutes   Cook Time: 15 Minutes   Serves: 4

Ingredients:

- 1 pound fresh scallops
- Zest and juice of 1 lemon
- 2 tablespoons chopped fresh dill
- 3 tablespoons olive oil
- Salt and pepper to taste
- 1 cup orzo, cooked
- 1 cucumber, diced
- 1 cup cherry tomatoes, halved
- 1/4 cup crumbled feta cheese

Directions:

1. Preheat one side of your Air Fryer to Air Broil at 400°F.

2. In a bowl, mix lemon zest, lemon juice, chopped dill, olive oil, salt, and pepper.
3. Toss scallops in the lemon-dill mixture and place them in one basket.
4. Air broil the scallops for 12-15 minutes, turning once, until they are opaque and slightly golden.
5. In a large bowl, combine cooked orzo, diced cucumber, halved cherry tomatoes, and crumbled feta cheese.
6. Serve the lemon-dill grilled scallops over a bed of orzo salad.

Nutritional Value (Amount per Serving):

Calories: 287; Fat: 13.32; Carb: 27.84; Protein: 16.35

Maple-Dijon Glazed Cedar Plank Salmon

Prep Time: 15 Minutes   Cook Time: 20 Minutes   Serves: 4

Ingredients:

- 4 salmon fillets
- 1/4 cup maple syrup
- 2 tablespoons Dijon mustard
- 1 tablespoon soy sauce
- 1 teaspoon minced garlic
- Salt and pepper to taste
- Cedar planks for grilling

Directions:

1. Preheat one side of your Air Fryer to Air Broil at 400°F.
2. In a bowl, whisk together maple syrup, Dijon mustard, soy sauce, minced garlic, salt, and pepper.
3. Brush the salmon fillets with the maple-Dijon glaze and place them on soaked cedar planks in one basket.
4. Air broil the salmon for 18-20 minutes until it's caramelized and cooked through.
5. At the same time, preheat the other side of the Air Fryer to Roast at 375°F.
6. Roast additional cedar planks for 10-12 minutes to intensify the smoky flavor.
7. Press the Smart Finish button.
8. Serve the maple-Dijon glazed cedar plank salmon on the roasted cedar planks.

Nutritional Value (Amount per Serving):

Calories: 164; Fat: 5.23; Carb: 19.95; Protein: 13.33

Grilled Swordfish Tacos with Pineapple Salsa

Prep Time: 20 Minutes   Cook Time: 15 Minutes   Serves: 4

Ingredients:

- 4 swordfish steaks
- 2 tablespoons olive oil
- 2 teaspoons chili powder
- 1 teaspoon cumin
- 1 teaspoon smoked paprika
- Salt and pepper to taste
- 8 small corn tortillas
- 2 cups pineapple, diced
- 1/2 red onion, finely chopped
- 1 jalapeño, seeded and minced
- 1/4 cup chopped fresh cilantro
- Lime wedges for serving

Directions:

1. Preheat one side of your Air Fryer to Air Fry at 375°F.
2. Brush swordfish steaks with olive oil and season with chili powder, cumin, smoked paprika, salt, and pepper. Place them in one basket.
3. Air fry the swordfish for 12-15 minutes until it's grilled and flakes easily.
4. At the same time, preheat the other side of the Air Fryer to Air Fry at 400°F.
5. Air fry corn tortillas for 2-3 minutes until they are warm and slightly crispy.
6. Press the Match Cook button.
7. In a bowl, combine diced pineapple, chopped red onion, minced jalapeño, and cilantro to make the salsa.
8. Serve grilled swordfish in warm tortillas topped with pineapple salsa and lime wedges.

Nutritional Value (Amount per Serving):

Calories: 760; Fat: 41.48; Carb: 46.76; Protein: 50.62

Coconut-Lime Grilled Mahi-Mahi Skewers

Prep Time: 20 Minutes   Cook Time: 10 Minutes   Serves: 4

Ingredients:

- 1.5 pounds mahi-mahi fillets, cut into cubes
- 1 cup coconut milk
- Zest and juice of 2 limes
- 2 tablespoons fish sauce
- 1 tablespoon soy sauce
- 1 tablespoon brown sugar
- 1 tablespoon grated ginger
- Wooden skewers, soaked in water

Directions:

1. Preheat one side of your Air Fryer to Air Broil at 400°F.
2. In a bowl, mix coconut milk, lime zest, lime juice, fish sauce, soy sauce,

brown sugar, and grated ginger.

3. Marinate mahi-mahi cubes in the coconut-lime mixture for at least 15 minutes.
4. Skewer the marinated fish onto soaked wooden skewers and place them in one basket.
5. Air broil the mahi-mahi skewers for 8-10 minutes until they are grilled and slightly caramelized.
6. Serve the coconut-lime grilled mahi-mahi skewers with your favorite dipping sauce.

Nutritional Value (Amount per Serving):

Calories: 465; Fat: 33.7; Carb: 8.69; Protein: 34.94

Orange-Glazed Lobster Tails with Herbed Quinoa

Prep Time: 25 Minutes   Cook Time: 15 Minutes   Serves: 4

Ingredients:

- 4 lobster tails, shell-on
- Zest and juice of 1 orange
- 1/4 cup honey
- 2 tablespoons soy sauce
- 1 tablespoon olive oil
- 1 teaspoon minced garlic
- Salt and pepper to taste
- 1 cup quinoa, cooked
- 2 tablespoons chopped fresh parsley
- 1 tablespoon chopped fresh chives

Directions:

1. Preheat one side of your Air Fryer to Roast at 400°F.
2. In a bowl, whisk together orange zest, orange juice, honey, soy sauce, olive oil, minced garlic, salt, and pepper.
3. Cut lobster tails down the middle, leaving the shell intact, and brush with the orange glaze. Place them in one basket.
4. Roast the lobster tails for 12-15 minutes until they are cooked and the glaze is caramelized.
5. At the same time, preheat the other side of the Air Fryer to Bake at 375°F.
6. Mix cooked quinoa with chopped parsley and chives, then bake for 10-12 minutes until it's warmed through.
7. Press the Smart Finish button.
8. Serve the orange-glazed lobster tails over a bed of herbed quinoa.

Nutritional Value (Amount per Serving):

Calories: 426; Fat: 8.64; Carb: 55.35; Protein: 32.19

Coconut-Curry Grilled Shrimp Skewers

Prep Time: 20 Minutes   Cook Time: 12 Minutes   Serves: 4

Ingredients:

- 1.5 pounds large shrimp, peeled and deveined
- 1 cup coconut milk
- 2 tablespoons red curry paste
- 1 tablespoon fish sauce
- 1 tablespoon brown sugar
- 1 tablespoon lime juice
- 2 teaspoons grated ginger
- Wooden skewers, soaked in water

Directions:

1. Preheat one side of your Air Fryer to Air Fry at 375°F.
2. In a bowl, combine coconut milk, red curry paste, fish sauce, brown sugar, lime juice, and grated ginger.
3. Marinate shrimp in the coconut-curry mixture for at least 15 minutes.
4. Skewer the marinated shrimp onto soaked wooden skewers and place them in one basket.
5. Air fry the shrimp skewers for 10-12 minutes until they are cooked through and slightly charred.
6. At the same time, preheat the other side of the Air Fryer to Dehydrate at 130°F.
7. Dehydrate lime slices for 2-3 hours until they become crispy.
8. Press the Smart Finish button.
9. Serve coconut-curry grilled shrimp skewers with a garnish of dehydrated lime slices.

Nutritional Value (Amount per Serving):

Calories: 175; Fat: 15.03; Carb: 10.2; Protein: 3.09

Teriyaki-Ginger Glazed Tuna Poke Bowls

Prep Time: 25 Minutes   Cook Time: 10 Minutes   Serves: 4

Ingredients:

- 1 pound sushi-grade tuna, cubed
- 1/4 cup soy sauce
- 2 tablespoons teriyaki sauce
- 1 tablespoon sesame oil
- 1 tablespoon rice vinegar
- 1 teaspoon grated ginger
- 2 cups cooked sushi rice
- 1 avocado, sliced
- 1 cucumber, julienned

- 1 carrot, shredded
- Sesame seeds and sliced green onions for garnish

Directions:

1. Preheat one side of your Air Fryer to Air Fry at 375°F.
2. In a bowl, mix soy sauce, teriyaki sauce, sesame oil, rice vinegar, and grated ginger.
3. Toss tuna cubes in the teriyaki-ginger glaze and place them in one basket.
4. Air fry the tuna for 8-10 minutes until it's lightly seared and still rare in the center.
5. At the same time, preheat the other side of the Air Fryer to Air Fry at 400°F.
6. Air fry sushi rice for 5-7 minutes until it's crispy and golden.
7. Press the Match Cook button.
8. Assemble poke bowls with crispy rice, teriyaki-ginger glazed tuna, sliced avocado, julienned cucumber, and shredded carrot.
9. Garnish with sesame seeds and sliced green onions.

Nutritional Value (Amount per Serving):

Calories: 582; Fat: 35.8; Carb: 41.72; Protein: 41.52

Garlic-Lemon Butter Lobster Tails with Herb-Infused Couscous

Prep Time: 20 Minutes   Cook Time: 15 Minutes   Serves: 4

Ingredients:

- 4 lobster tails, shell-on
- 1/2 cup unsalted butter, melted
- 4 cloves garlic, minced
- Zest and juice of 2 lemons
- Salt and pepper to taste
- 1.5 cups couscous, cooked
- 2 tablespoons chopped fresh parsley
- 1 tablespoon chopped fresh dill

Directions:

1. Preheat one side of your Air Fryer to Air Broil at 400°F.
2. Cut lobster tails down the middle, leaving the shell intact.
3. In a bowl, mix melted butter, minced garlic, lemon zest, lemon juice, salt, and pepper.
4. Brush lobster tails with the garlic-lemon butter mixture and place them in one basket.
5. Air broil the lobster tails for 12-15 minutes until they are cooked and the shell is lightly charred.
6. At the same time, preheat the other side of the Air Fryer to Roast at 375°F.
7. Roast cooked couscous for 8-10 minutes until it's warmed through.

8. Press the Smart Finish button.
9. Serve garlic-lemon butter lobster tails over a bed of herb-infused couscous, garnished with chopped parsley and dill.

Nutritional Value (Amount per Serving):

Calories: 341; Fat: 17; Carb: 18.41; Protein: 28.76

Spicy Mango-Glazed Red Snapper with Cilantro-Lime Rice

Prep Time: 15 Minutes   Cook Time: 20 Minutes   Serves: 4

Ingredients:

- 4 red snapper fillets
- 1 cup mango puree
- 2 tablespoons hot sauce
- 1/4 cup honey
- 1 tablespoon soy sauce
- 1 teaspoon minced garlic
- Salt and pepper to taste
- 1 cup white rice, cooked
- 2 tablespoons chopped fresh cilantro
- Zest and juice of 1 lime

Directions:

1. Preheat one side of your Air Fryer to Roast at 400°F.
2. In a bowl, combine mango puree, hot sauce, honey, soy sauce, minced garlic, salt, and pepper.
3. Brush red snapper fillets with the spicy mango glaze and place them in one basket.
4. Roast the red snapper for 18-20 minutes until it's glazed and cooked through.
5. At the same time, preheat the other side of the Air Fryer to Bake at 375°F.
6. Mix cooked white rice with chopped cilantro, lime zest, and lime juice. Bake for 10-12 minutes until it's heated through.
7. Press the Smart Finish button.
8. Serve spicy mango-glazed red snapper over a bed of cilantro-lime rice.

Nutritional Value (Amount per Serving):

Calories: 333; Fat: 1.26; Carb: 78.03; Protein: 4.67

Chimichurri-Grilled Mussels with Crispy Garlic Bread

Prep Time: 20 Minutes   Cook Time: 10 Minutes   Serves: 4

Ingredients:

- 2 pounds mussels, cleaned and debearded
- 1 cup fresh parsley, finely chopped

- 1/4 cup red wine vinegar
- 2 tablespoons fresh oregano, chopped
- 4 cloves garlic, minced
- 1 teaspoon red pepper flakes
- 1/2 cup olive oil
- Salt and pepper to taste
- 1 baguette, sliced
- 2 tablespoons unsalted butter, melted

Directions:

1. Preheat one side of your Air Fryer to Air Fry at 375°F.
2. In a bowl, combine chopped parsley, red wine vinegar, chopped oregano, minced garlic, red pepper flakes, olive oil, salt, and pepper.
3. Toss mussels in the chimichurri mixture and place them in one basket.
4. Air fry the mussels for 8-10 minutes until they open and are cooked through.
5. At the same time, preheat the other side of the Air Fryer to Roast at 400°F.
6. Brush baguette slices with melted butter and roast for 3-5 minutes until they are crispy and golden.
7. Press the Smart Finish button.
8. Serve chimichurri-grilled mussels with crispy garlic bread on the side.

Nutritional Value (Amount per Serving):

Calories: 515; Fat: 38.07; Carb: 13.1; Protein: 29.56

Chapter 5: Vegetables and Sides

Crispy Potato Wedges and Rosemary Lemon Chicken Bites

Prep Time: 20 Minutes   Cook Time: 25 Minutes   Serves: 4

Ingredients:

- 4 medium russet potatoes, cut into wedges
- 3 tablespoons olive oil
- 1 teaspoon garlic powder
- 1 teaspoon paprika
- Salt and black pepper to taste
- 1 lb boneless, skinless chicken breasts, cut into bite-sized pieces
- 2 tablespoons olive oil
- 1 tablespoon fresh rosemary, chopped
- Zest of 1 lemon
- Salt and black pepper to taste

Directions:

1. Preheat one side of your Air Fryer to Air Fry at 400°F.
2. In a bowl, toss potato wedges with olive oil, garlic powder, paprika, salt, and pepper.
3. Place the seasoned potato wedges in one basket.
4. Preheat the other side of the Air Fryer to Air Fry at 375°F.
5. In a separate bowl, combine chicken pieces with olive oil, chopped rosemary, lemon zest, salt, and pepper.
6. Place the seasoned chicken bites in the second basket.
7. Press the Match Cook button.
8. Air fry both the potato wedges and chicken bites for 20-25 minutes, shaking the baskets halfway through, until the potatoes are golden and the chicken is cooked through.
9. Serve the dual delight crispy potato wedges and rosemary lemon chicken bites hot as a satisfying combo.

Nutritional Value (Amount per Serving):

Calories: 654; Fat: 23.8; Carb: 94.29; Protein: 19.12

Honey Glazed Carrots and Parmesan Zucchini Fries

Prep Time: 15 Minutes   Cook Time: 20 Minutes   Serves: 4

Ingredients:

- 1 lb baby carrots, peeled
- 3 tablespoons honey

- 2 tablespoons olive oil
- 1 teaspoon ground ginger
- Salt and pepper to taste
- 3 medium zucchinis, cut into fries
- 1/2 cup grated Parmesan cheese
- 2 tablespoons olive oil
- 1 teaspoon garlic powder
- Salt and pepper to taste

Directions:

1. Preheat one side of your Air Fryer to Roast at 375°F.
2. In a bowl, mix baby carrots with honey, olive oil, ground ginger, salt, and pepper.
3. Place the honey glazed carrots in one basket.
4. Preheat the other side of the Air Fryer to Air Fry at 400°F.
5. In a separate bowl, coat zucchini fries with Parmesan cheese, olive oil, garlic powder, salt, and pepper.
6. Place the Parmesan zucchini fries in the second basket.
7. Press the Smart Finish button.
8. Roast the honey glazed carrots and air fry the Parmesan zucchini fries for 18-20 minutes, shaking the baskets halfway through.
9. Serve the duo veggie medley hot, combining the honey glazed carrots and Parmesan zucchini fries for a balanced side dish.

Nutritional Value (Amount per Serving):

Calories: 274; Fat: 17.23; Carb: 27.33; Protein: 5.17

Crunch Fish and Sweet Potato Chips

Prep Time: 20 Minutes   Cook Time: 25 Minutes   Serves: 4

Ingredients:

- 1 lb white fish fillets (such as cod or tilapia)
- 1 cup breadcrumbs
- 2 tablespoons flour
- 2 eggs, beaten
- Salt and pepper to taste
- 2 large sweet potatoes, cut into thin chips
- 3 tablespoons olive oil
- 1 teaspoon smoked paprika
- Salt to taste

Directions:

1. Preheat one side of your Air Fryer to Air Fry at 375°F.

2. Coat fish fillets in flour, dip in beaten eggs, then coat with breadcrumbs seasoned with salt and pepper.
3. Place the breaded fish fillets in one basket.
4. Preheat the other side of the Air Fryer to Air Fry at 400°F.
5. In a separate bowl, toss sweet potato chips with olive oil, smoked paprika, and salt.
6. Place the seasoned sweet potato chips in the second basket.
7. Press the Match Cook button.
8. Air fry both the fish and sweet potato chips for 20-25 minutes, shaking the baskets halfway through, until the fish is crispy and the sweet potato chips are golden.
9. Serve the dual crunch fish and sweet potato chips hot with your favorite dipping sauce.

Nutritional Value (Amount per Serving):

Calories: 334; Fat: 15.4; Carb: 44.02; Protein: 7.82

Tangy Teriyaki Shrimp Skewers and Pineapple Salsa

Prep Time: 15 Minutes   Cook Time: 10 Minutes   Serves: 4

Ingredients:

- 1 lb large shrimp, peeled and deveined
- 1/4 cup teriyaki sauce
- 2 tablespoons olive oil
- 1 teaspoon garlic powder
- 1 teaspoon sesame seeds
- 1 cup diced fresh pineapple
- 1/4 cup red onion, finely chopped
- 1/4 cup cilantro, chopped
- Juice of 1 lime
- Salt and pepper to taste

Directions:

1. Preheat one side of your Air Fryer to Air Broil at 400°F.
2. In a bowl, marinate shrimp with teriyaki sauce, olive oil, garlic powder, and sesame seeds.
3. Thread marinated shrimp onto skewers and place them in one basket.
4. Preheat the other side of the Air Fryer to Air Fry at 375°F.
5. In a separate bowl, mix diced pineapple, red onion, cilantro, lime juice, salt, and pepper to make the salsa.
6. Place the pineapple salsa in the second basket.
7. Press the Smart Finish button.
8. Air broil the shrimp skewers and air fry the pineapple salsa for 8-10 minutes, turning the shrimp halfway through, until the shrimp are cooked through and slightly charred.
9. Serve the tangy teriyaki shrimp skewers with a side of refreshing pineapple salsa.

Nutritional Value (Amount per Serving):

Calories: 145; Fat: 7.45; Carb: 18.56; Protein: 2.66

Roasted Herb Potatoes and Lemon Garlic Chicken Thighs

Prep Time: 20 Minutes   Cook Time: 30 Minutes   Serves: 4

Ingredients:

- 1.5 lbs baby potatoes, halved
- 3 tablespoons olive oil
- 1 teaspoon dried thyme
- 1 teaspoon dried rosemary
- Salt and black pepper to taste
- 4 bone-in, skin-on chicken thighs
- 2 tablespoons olive oil
- Zest and juice of 1 lemon
- 3 cloves garlic, minced
- 1 teaspoon dried oregano
- Salt and black pepper to taste

Directions:

1. Preheat one side of your Air Fryer to Roast at 400°F.
2. Toss halved baby potatoes with olive oil, dried thyme, dried rosemary, salt, and black pepper.
3. Place the seasoned potatoes in one basket.
4. Preheat the other side of the Air Fryer to Air Fry at 375°F.
5. In a separate bowl, coat chicken thighs with olive oil, lemon zest, lemon juice, minced garlic, dried oregano, salt, and black pepper.
6. Place the seasoned chicken thighs in the second basket.
7. Press the Smart Finish button.
8. Roast the herb potatoes and air fry the lemon garlic chicken thighs for 28-30 minutes, shaking the baskets halfway through, until the potatoes are crispy and the chicken is golden and cooked through.
9. Serve the dual roasted herb potatoes and lemon garlic chicken thighs hot as a hearty meal.

Nutritional Value (Amount per Serving):

Calories: 1294; Fat: 117.45; Carb: 35.47; Protein: 25.84

Crispy Brussel Sprouts and Honey Glazed Salmon

Prep Time: 20 Minutes   Cook Time: 20 Minutes   Serves: 4

Ingredients:

- 1 lb Brussels sprouts, trimmed and halved
- 3 tablespoons olive oil

- 1 teaspoon garlic powder
- 1/4 cup grated Parmesan cheese
- Salt and black pepper to taste
- 4 salmon fillets
- 1/4 cup honey
- 2 tablespoons soy sauce
- 1 tablespoon Dijon mustard
- 1 teaspoon minced ginger
- Salt and black pepper to taste

Directions:

1. Preheat one side of your Air Fryer to Air Fry at 375°F.
2. Toss Brussels sprouts with olive oil, garlic powder, grated Parmesan, salt, and black pepper.
3. Place the seasoned Brussels sprouts in one basket.
4. Preheat the other side of the Air Fryer to Air Fry at 400°F.
5. In a separate bowl, whisk together honey, soy sauce, Dijon mustard, minced ginger, salt, and black pepper to make the glaze.
6. Coat salmon fillets with the honey glaze and place them in the second basket.
7. Press the Match Cook button.
8. Air fry both the Brussels sprouts and salmon for 18-20 minutes, shaking the baskets halfway through, until the Brussels sprouts are crispy and the salmon is glazed and cooked through.
9. Serve the dual crispy Brussels sprouts and honey glazed salmon hot for a delicious pairing.

Nutritional Value (Amount per Serving):

Calories: 353; Fat: 17.9; Carb: 33.48; Protein: 18.67

Herb-Crusted Cauliflower and BBQ Chicken Wings

Prep Time: 20 Minutes   Cook Time: 25 Minutes   Serves: 4

Ingredients:

- 1 head cauliflower, cut into florets
- 3 tablespoons olive oil
- 1 teaspoon dried thyme
- 1 teaspoon dried rosemary
- 1/4 cup breadcrumbs
- Salt and black pepper to taste
- 2 lbs chicken wings
- 1/2 cup BBQ sauce
- 2 tablespoons olive oil
- 1 teaspoon smoked paprika
- Salt and black pepper to taste

Directions:

1. Preheat one side of your Air Fryer to Roast at 375°F.

2. Toss cauliflower florets with olive oil, dried thyme, dried rosemary, breadcrumbs, salt, and black pepper.
3. Place the seasoned cauliflower in one basket.
4. Preheat the other side of the Air Fryer to Air Fry at 400°F.
5. In a separate bowl, mix chicken wings with BBQ sauce, olive oil, smoked paprika, salt, and black pepper.
6. Place the BBQ chicken wings in the second basket.
7. Press the Smart Finish button.
8. Roast the herb-crusted cauliflower and air fry the BBQ chicken wings for 22-25 minutes, shaking the baskets halfway through, until the cauliflower is golden and the chicken wings are crispy and glazed.
9. Serve the dual roasted herb-crusted cauliflower and BBQ chicken wings hot for a satisfying meal.

Nutritional Value (Amount per Serving):

Calories: 472; Fat: 25.28; Carb: 8; Protein: 52.15

Herb-Infused Roasted Bell Peppers and Pesto Zucchini Noodles

Prep Time: 15 Minutes   Cook Time: 20 Minutes   Serves: 4

Ingredients:

- 3 bell peppers (red, yellow, or orange), sliced
- 3 tablespoons olive oil
- 1 teaspoon dried basil
- 1 teaspoon dried oregano
- Salt and black pepper to taste
- 4 medium zucchinis, spiralized
- 1/2 cup homemade or store-bought pesto
- 1/4 cup pine nuts, toasted
- Grated Parmesan cheese for garnishf

Directions:

1. Preheat one side of your Air Fryer to Roast at 375°F.
2. Toss bell pepper slices with olive oil, dried basil, dried oregano, salt, and black pepper.
3. Place the seasoned bell peppers in one basket.
4. Preheat the other side of the Air Fryer to Air Fry at 400°F.
5. In a separate bowl, mix spiralized zucchini with pesto.
6. Place the pesto-coated zucchini noodles in the second basket.
7. Press the Smart Finish button.
8. Roast the herb-infused bell peppers and air fry the pesto zucchini noodles

for 18-20 minutes, shaking the baskets halfway through.

9. Garnish the pesto zucchini noodles with toasted pine nuts and grated Parmesan before serving.

Nutritional Value (Amount per Serving):

Calories: 196; Fat: 16.32; Carb: 12.22; Protein: 3.41

Maple Glazed Acorn Squash and Cranberry Walnut Quinoa

Prep Time: 15 Minutes   Cook Time: 30 Minutes   Serves: 4

Ingredients:

- 2 acorn squashes, sliced
- 3 tablespoons maple syrup
- 2 tablespoons melted butter
- 1 teaspoon cinnamon
- Salt to taste
- 1 cup quinoa, cooked
- 1/2 cup dried cranberries
- 1/2 cup chopped walnuts
- Zest of 1 orange
- Salt and black pepper to taste

Directions:

1. Preheat one side of your Air Fryer to Roast at 375°F.
2. Toss acorn squash slices with maple syrup, melted butter, cinnamon, and salt.
3. Place the seasoned acorn squash in one basket.
4. Preheat the other side of the Air Fryer to Air Fry at 400°F.
5. In a separate bowl, mix cooked quinoa with dried cranberries, chopped walnuts, orange zest, salt, and black pepper.
6. Place the cranberry walnut quinoa in the second basket.
7. Press the Smart Finish button.
8. Roast the maple glazed acorn squash and air fry the cranberry walnut quinoa for 28-30 minutes, shaking the baskets halfway through.
9. Serve the dual maple glazed acorn squash and cranberry walnut quinoa as a wholesome side dish.

Nutritional Value (Amount per Serving):

Calories: 452; Fat: 15.22; Carb: 74.2; Protein: 9.99

Spiced Butternut Squash and Quinoa Stuffed Portobello Mushrooms

Prep Time: 20 Minutes   Cook Time: 25 Minutes   Serves: 4

Ingredients:

- 1 small butternut squash, peeled and diced

- 3 tablespoons olive oil
- 1 teaspoon ground cumin
- 1 teaspoon ground coriander
- 1/2 teaspoon smoked paprika
- Salt and black pepper to taste
- 4 large portobello mushrooms, stems removed
- 1 cup quinoa, cooked
- 1/2 cup feta cheese, crumbled
- 1/4 cup chopped fresh parsley
- Zest of 1 lemon
- Salt and black pepper to taste

Directions:

1. Preheat one side of your Air Fryer to Roast at 375°F.
2. Toss diced butternut squash with olive oil, ground cumin, ground coriander, smoked paprika, salt, and black pepper.
3. Place the seasoned butternut squash in one basket.
4. Preheat the other side of the Air Fryer to Air Fry at 400°F.
5. In a separate bowl, mix cooked quinoa with feta cheese, chopped fresh parsley, lemon zest, salt, and black pepper.
6. Stuff portobello mushrooms with the quinoa mixture and place them in the second basket.
7. Press the Smart Finish button.
8. Roast the spiced butternut squash and air fry the quinoa stuffed portobello mushrooms for 22-25 minutes, shaking the baskets halfway through.
9. Serve the dual roasted spiced butternut squash and quinoa stuffed portobello mushrooms for a hearty and satisfying side.

Nutritional Value (Amount per Serving):

Calories: 338; Fat: 17.27; Carb: 37.14; Protein: 11.32

Balsamic Glazed Brussels Sprouts and Mediterranean Chickpea Salad

Prep Time: 15 Minutes   Cook Time: 20 Minutes   Serves: 4

Ingredients:

- 1 lb Brussels sprouts, trimmed and halved
- 3 tablespoons balsamic glaze
- 2 tablespoons olive oil
- 1 teaspoon honey
- Salt and black pepper to taste
- 1 can (15 oz) chickpeas, drained and rinsed

- 1 cup cherry tomatoes, halved
- 1 cucumber, diced
- 1/4 cup Kalamata olives, sliced
- 1/4 cup feta cheese, crumbled
- 2 tablespoons red onion, finely chopped
- 2 tablespoons fresh parsley, chopped
- Juice of 1 lemon
- 3 tablespoons extra-virgin olive oil
- Salt and black pepper to taste

Directions:

1. Preheat one side of your Air Fryer to Air Fry at 375°F.
2. Toss Brussels sprouts with balsamic glaze, olive oil, honey, salt, and black pepper. Place the seasoned Brussels sprouts in one basket.
3. Preheat the other side of the Air Fryer to Air Fry at 400°F.
4. In a large bowl, combine chickpeas, cherry tomatoes, cucumber, Kalamata olives, feta cheese, red onion, fresh parsley, lemon juice, extra-virgin olive oil, salt, and black pepper to make the Mediterranean chickpea salad.
5. Place the chickpea salad in the second basket.
6. Press the Match Cook button.
7. Air fry the balsamic glazed Brussels sprouts and the Mediterranean chickpea salad for 18-20 minutes, shaking the baskets halfway through.
8. Serve the dual balsamic glazed Brussels sprouts and Mediterranean chickpea salad for a delightful and wholesome side.

Nutritional Value (Amount per Serving):

Calories: 314; Fat: 16.39; Carb: 35.47; Protein: 11.61

Garlic Parmesan Green Beans and Balsamic Glazed Tomato Bruschetta

Prep Time: 15 Minutes   Cook Time: 15 Minutes   Serves: 4

Ingredients:

- 1 lb fresh green beans, ends trimmed
- 3 tablespoons olive oil
- 3 cloves garlic, minced
- 1/4 cup grated Parmesan cheese
- Salt and black pepper to taste
- 2 cups cherry tomatoes, quartered
- 2 tablespoons balsamic glaze
- 2 tablespoons fresh basil, chopped
- 1 clove garlic, minced

- Salt and black pepper to taste

Directions:

1. Preheat one side of your Air Fryer to Bake at 375°F.
2. Toss green beans with olive oil, minced garlic, grated Parmesan, salt, and black pepper.
3. Place the seasoned green beans in one basket.
4. Preheat the other side of the Air Fryer to Air Fry at 400°F.
5. In a bowl, mix quartered cherry tomatoes, balsamic glaze, chopped fresh basil, minced garlic, salt, and black pepper to make the balsamic glazed tomato bruschetta.
6. Place the tomato bruschetta in the second basket.
7. Press the Smart Finish button.
8. Bake the garlic Parmesan green beans and air fry the balsamic glazed tomato bruschetta for 12-15 minutes, shaking the baskets halfway through.
9. Serve the dual garlic Parmesan air-baked green beans and balsamic glazed tomato bruschetta for a flavorful and vibrant side.

Nutritional Value (Amount per Serving):

Calories: 168; Fat: 12.57; Carb: 11.87; Protein: 4.39

Sesame Ginger Broccoli and Coconut Lime Jasmine Rice

Prep Time: 15 Minutes   Cook Time: 20 Minutes   Serves: 4

Ingredients:

- 1 lb broccoli florets
- 3 tablespoons soy sauce
- 2 tablespoons sesame oil
- 1 tablespoon rice vinegar
- 1 tablespoon honey
- 1 teaspoon grated ginger
- 1 teaspoon sesame seeds
- 2 cups jasmine rice, cooked
- 1 cup coconut milk
- Zest and juice of 1 lime
- 2 tablespoons fresh cilantro, chopped
- Salt to taste

Directions:

1. Preheat one side of your Air Fryer to Air Fry at 375°F.
2. In a bowl, whisk together soy sauce, sesame oil, rice vinegar, honey, grated ginger, and sesame seeds to make the sesame ginger sauce.
3. Toss broccoli florets with the sesame ginger sauce.
4. Place the seasoned broccoli in one basket.
5. Preheat the other side of the Air Fryer to Air Fry at 400°F.
6. In a separate bowl, combine cooked jasmine rice with coconut milk, lime

zest, lime juice, fresh cilantro, and salt to make the coconut lime jasmine rice.

7. Place the coconut lime jasmine rice in the second basket.
8. Press the Match Cook button.
9. Air fry the sesame ginger broccoli and coconut lime jasmine rice for 18-20 minutes, shaking the baskets halfway through.
10. Serve the dual sesame ginger broccoli and coconut lime jasmine rice for an aromatic and satisfying side.

Nutritional Value (Amount per Serving):

Calories: 365; Fat: 24.53; Carb: 32.5; Protein: 9.31

Cauliflower Steaks and Caprese Stuffed Portobello Mushrooms

Prep Time: 20 Minutes   Cook Time: 25 Minutes   Serves: 4

Ingredients:

- 1 large head cauliflower, sliced into steaks
- 1/2 cup homemade or store-bought pesto
- 1/4 cup pine nuts, toasted
- Salt and black pepper to taste
- 4 large portobello mushrooms, stems removed
- 1 cup grape tomatoes, halved
- 1 cup fresh mozzarella balls, halved
- 1/4 cup fresh basil leaves, torn
- 2 tablespoons balsamic glaze
- Salt and black pepper to taste

Directions:

1. Preheat one side of your Air Fryer to Roast at 375°F.
2. Brush cauliflower steaks with pesto and sprinkle with toasted pine nuts, salt, and black pepper.
3. Place the pesto-roasted cauliflower steaks in one basket.
4. Preheat the other side of the Air Fryer to Air Fry at 400°F.
5. In a bowl, combine halved grape tomatoes, fresh mozzarella balls, torn basil leaves, balsamic glaze, salt, and black pepper to make the Caprese stuffing.
6. Stuff portobello mushrooms with the Caprese mixture and place them in the second basket.
7. Press the Smart Finish button.
8. Roast the pesto-roasted cauliflower steaks and air fry the Caprese stuffed portobello mushrooms for 22-25 minutes, shaking the baskets halfway

through.

9. Serve the dual pesto-roasted cauliflower steaks and Caprese stuffed portobello mushrooms for a flavorful and satisfying side.

Nutritional Value (Amount per Serving):

Calories: 150; Fat: 6.59; Carb: 21.76; Protein: 5.87

Roasted Garlic Parmesan Brussels Sprouts with Bacon

Prep Time: 15 Minutes   Cook Time: 20 Minutes   Serves: 4

Ingredients:

- 1 lb Brussels sprouts, trimmed and halved
- 4 slices bacon, cooked and crumbled
- 3 tablespoons olive oil
- 3 cloves garlic, minced
- 1/4 cup grated Parmesan cheese
- Salt and black pepper to taste

Directions:

1. Preheat one side of your Air Fryer to Air Fry at 375°F.
2. Press the Smart Finish button.
3. In a bowl, toss Brussels sprouts with olive oil, minced garlic, salt, and black pepper.
4. Place the seasoned Brussels sprouts in one basket.
5. Air fry for 18-20 minutes, shaking the basket halfway through, until the Brussels sprouts are golden and crispy.
6. Once done, switch the Air Fryer to Air Broil at 400°F.
7. Sprinkle the cooked bacon and Parmesan cheese over the Brussels sprouts.
8. Air broil for an additional 2-3 minutes until the cheese is melted and bubbly.
9. Serve hot as a flavorful side dish.

Nutritional Value (Amount per Serving):

Calories: 278; Fat: 22.45; Carb: 13.04; Protein: 9.24

Chapter 6: Appetizers and Snacks

Southwest Egg Rolls & Stuffed Jalapeños

Prep Time: 30 Minutes   Cook Time: 20 Minutes   Serves: 4

Ingredients:

- 8 egg roll wrappers
- 1 cup cooked chicken, shredded
- 1/2 cup black beans, drained and rinsed
- 1/2 cup corn kernels
- 1/2 cup diced bell peppers (mix of colors)
- 1/2 cup shredded Monterey Jack cheese
- 1 teaspoon cumin
- 1 teaspoon chili powder
- 1/2 teaspoon garlic powder
- 1/4 cup chopped cilantro
- Salsa for dipping
- 8 large jalapeño peppers, halved and seeded
- 1 cup cream cheese, softened
- 1 cup shredded pepper jack cheese
- 1/2 cup cooked and crumbled chorizo
- Chopped fresh cilantro for garnish

Directions:

1. Preheat one side of your Air Fryer to Air Fry at 375°F for southwest egg rolls and the other side at 400°F for stuffed jalapeños.
2. In a bowl, mix shredded chicken, black beans, corn, bell peppers, Monterey Jack cheese, cumin, chili powder, garlic powder, and cilantro.
3. Place a spoonful of the mixture in the center of each egg roll wrapper. Roll according to package instructions.
4. Arrange the egg rolls in one basket.
5. In another bowl, combine cream cheese, pepper jack cheese, and cooked chorizo.
6. Fill each jalapeño half with the cream cheese mixture.
7. Place the stuffed jalapeños in the second basket.
8. Press the Match Cook button.
9. Air fry both baskets for 20 minutes, shaking halfway through, until the egg rolls are golden and the jalapeños are tender.
10. Swap the baskets after 10 minutes for even cooking.
11. Serve hot with salsa for the egg rolls and garnish the stuffed jalapeños with cilantro.

Nutritional Value (Amount per Serving):

Calories: 983; Fat: 61.17; Carb: 58.94; Protein: 50.02

Caprese Skewers & Crispy Prosciutto-Wrapped Asparagus

Prep Time: 25 Minutes   Cook Time: 15 Minutes   Serves: 4

Ingredients:

- 16 cherry tomatoes
- 16 fresh mozzarella balls
- 16 fresh basil leaves
- Balsamic glaze for drizzling
- 16 asparagus spears, trimmed
- 8 slices prosciutto, halved
- Olive oil for brushing
- Lemon wedges for serving

Directions:

1. Preheat one side of your Air Fryer to Air Broil at 400°F for caprese skewers and Air Fry at 375°F for prosciutto-wrapped asparagus.
2. Thread cherry tomatoes, mozzarella balls, and basil leaves onto skewers.
3. Arrange the caprese skewers in one basket.
4. Wrap each asparagus spear with a half-slice of prosciutto.
5. Place the prosciutto-wrapped asparagus in the second basket.
6. Press the Smart Finish button.
7. Air broil the caprese skewers for 10 minutes and air fry the asparagus for 15 minutes, both shaking halfway through.
8. Drizzle balsamic glaze over the caprese skewers and serve them alongside crispy prosciutto-wrapped asparagus.
9. Garnish with lemon wedges for a burst of freshness.

Nutritional Value (Amount per Serving):

Calories: 605; Fat: 26.65; Carb: 23.33; Protein: 72.41

Avocado Fries & Onion Rings

Prep Time: 20 Minutes   Cook Time: 15 Minutes   Serves: 4

Ingredients:

- 2 large avocados, sliced into fries
- 1 cup breadcrumbs
- 1 teaspoon garlic powder
- 1 teaspoon paprika

- Salt and pepper to taste
- Lime wedges for serving
- 2 large onions, sliced into rings
- 1 cup buttermilk
- 1 cup flour
- 1 teaspoon garlic powder
- 1 teaspoon onion powder
- 1/2 teaspoon cayenne pepper
- Salt and pepper to taste

Directions:

1. Preheat one side of your Air Fryer to Air Fry at 375°F for avocado fries and the other side at 400°F for onion rings.
2. In a bowl, combine breadcrumbs, garlic powder, paprika, salt, and pepper.
3. Dredge avocado slices in the breadcrumb mixture.
4. Place the avocado fries in one basket.
5. In another bowl, soak onion rings in buttermilk for 15 minutes.
6. In a separate bowl, mix flour, garlic powder, onion powder, cayenne pepper, salt, and pepper.
7. Coat soaked onion rings in the flour mixture.
8. Arrange the onion rings in the second basket.
9. Press the Match Cook button.
10. Air fry both baskets for 15 minutes, shaking halfway through, until the avocado fries are crispy and the onion rings are golden.
11. Swap the baskets after 7 minutes for even cooking.
12. Serve hot with lime wedges for the avocado fries and your favorite dipping sauce for the onion rings.

Nutritional Value (Amount per Serving):

Calories: 322; Fat: 15.76; Carb: 40.73; Protein: 8.22

Mediterranean Stuffed Mushrooms & Greek Zucchini Chips

Prep Time: 25 Minutes   Cook Time: 20 Minutes   Serves: 4

Ingredients:

- 16 large mushrooms, stems removed
- 1 cup feta cheese, crumbled
- 1/2 cup sun-dried tomatoes, chopped
- 1/4 cup Kalamata olives, chopped
- 1/4 cup fresh parsley, chopped
- Olive oil for drizzling

- 2 large zucchinis, thinly sliced
- 1/4 cup olive oil
- 1 teaspoon dried oregano
- 1 teaspoon garlic powder
- Salt and pepper to taste
- Tzatziki sauce for dipping

Directions:

1. Preheat one side of your Air Fryer to Air Fry at 375°F for Mediterranean stuffed mushrooms and the other side at 400°F for Greek zucchini chips.
2. In a bowl, mix feta cheese, sun-dried tomatoes, olives, and parsley.
3. Fill each mushroom cap with the feta mixture.
4. Place the stuffed mushrooms in one basket.
5. In another bowl, toss zucchini slices with olive oil, dried oregano, garlic powder, salt, and pepper.
6. Arrange the seasoned zucchini slices in the second basket.
7. Press the Match Cook button.
8. Air fry both baskets for 20 minutes, shaking halfway through, until the mushrooms are tender and the zucchini chips are golden.
9. Swap the baskets after 10 minutes for even cooking.
10. Drizzle olive oil over the stuffed mushrooms and serve with tzatziki sauce alongside crispy Greek zucchini chips.

Nutritional Value (Amount per Serving):

Calories: 427; Fat: 37.73; Carb: 11.34; Protein: 14.47

Sesame Ginger Chicken Wings & Coconut Shrimp

Prep Time: 25 Minutes   Cook Time: 20 Minutes   Serves: 4

Ingredients:

- 1 lb chicken wings
- 1/4 cup soy sauce
- 2 tablespoons honey
- 1 tablespoon sesame oil
- 1 tablespoon grated ginger
- 1 tablespoon sesame seeds
- Chopped green onions for garnish
- 1 lb large shrimp, peeled and deveined
- 1 cup shredded coconut
- 1 cup panko breadcrumbs
- 2 eggs, beaten
- Sweet chili sauce for dipping

Directions:

1. Preheat one side of your Air Fryer to Air Fry at 400°F for sesame ginger chicken wings and the other side at 375°F for coconut shrimp.
2. In a bowl, mix soy sauce, honey, sesame oil, ginger, and sesame seeds. Toss chicken wings in this mixture.
3. Place the marinated chicken wings in one basket.
4. In another bowl, combine shredded coconut and panko breadcrumbs.
5. Dip each shrimp in beaten eggs, then coat with the coconut-breadcrumb mixture.
6. Arrange the coated shrimp in the second basket.
7. Press the Match Cook button.
8. Air fry both baskets for 20 minutes, shaking halfway through, until the chicken wings are glazed and the coconut shrimp are golden and crispy.
9. Swap the baskets after 10 minutes for even cooking.
10. Garnish chicken wings with chopped green onions and serve with sweet chili sauce.

Nutritional Value (Amount per Serving):

Calories: 389; Fat: 16.74; Carb: 25.95; Protein: 32.94

Tex-Mex Stuffed Peppers & Chili Cheese Fries

Prep Time: 30 Minutes   Cook Time: 25 Minutes   Serves: 4

Ingredients:

- 4 large bell peppers, halved and seeded
- 1 lb ground beef
- 1 cup cooked rice
- 1 cup black beans, drained and rinsed
- 1 cup corn kernels
- 1 cup salsa
- 1 tablespoon taco seasoning
- Shredded cheddar cheese for topping
- 4 large potatoes, cut into fries
- 1 cup chili (canned or homemade)
- 1 cup shredded Monterey Jack cheese
- Sliced jalapeños for garnish

Directions:

1. Preheat one side of your Air Fryer to Air Fry at 375°F for Tex-Mex stuffed peppers and the other side at 400°F for chili cheese fries.
2. In a skillet, cook ground beef until browned. Drain excess fat.
3. In a bowl, mix cooked beef, rice, black beans, corn, salsa, and taco

seasoning.

4. Fill each bell pepper half with the Tex-Mex mixture.
5. Place the stuffed peppers in one basket.
6. In another bowl, toss potato fries with chili and shredded Monterey Jack cheese.
7. Arrange the chili cheese fries in the second basket.
8. Press the Match Cook button.
9. Air fry both baskets for 25 minutes, shaking halfway through, until the stuffed peppers are tender, and the chili cheese fries are golden and cheesy.
10. Swap the baskets after 15 minutes for even cooking.
11. Garnish the stuffed peppers with shredded cheddar cheese and top the chili cheese fries with sliced jalapeños.

Nutritional Value (Amount per Serving):

Calories: 993; Fat: 50.26; Carb: 96.39; Protein: 58.12

Cajun Crab Cakes & Lemon Herb Zucchini Chips

Prep Time: 30 Minutes   Cook Time: 20 Minutes   Serves: 4

Ingredients:

- 1 lb lump crabmeat
- 1/2 cup mayonnaise
- 1/4 cup breadcrumbs
- 2 tablespoons Dijon mustard
- 1 tablespoon Old Bay seasoning
- 1 tablespoon lemon juice
- 1 egg, beaten
- Olive oil for brushing
- 2 large zucchinis, thinly sliced
- 1/4 cup olive oil
- 1 tablespoon lemon zest
- 1 tablespoon fresh herbs (such as parsley or thyme), chopped
- Salt and pepper to taste
- Garlic aioli for dipping

Directions:

1. Preheat one side of your Air Fryer to Air Fry at 375°F for Cajun crab cakes and the other side at 400°F for lemon herb zucchini chips.
2. In a bowl, mix crabmeat, mayonnaise, breadcrumbs, Dijon mustard, Old Bay seasoning, lemon juice, and beaten egg.
3. Form the mixture into crab cakes and place them in one basket.
4. In another bowl, toss zucchini slices with olive oil, lemon zest, fresh herbs,

salt, and pepper.

5. Arrange the seasoned zucchini chips in the second basket.
6. Press the Match Cook button.
7. Air fry both baskets for 20 minutes, shaking halfway through, until the crab cakes are golden and the zucchini chips are crispy.
8. Swap the baskets after 10 minutes for even cooking.
9. Brush crab cakes with olive oil before serving and dip zucchini chips in garlic aioli.

Nutritional Value (Amount per Serving):

Calories: 414; Fat: 40.55; Carb: 4.26; Protein: 9.42

Buffalo Chicken Quesadillas & Loaded Nacho Bites

Prep Time: 25 Minutes   Cook Time: 20 Minutes   Serves: 4

Ingredients:

- 2 cups cooked chicken, shredded
- 1/2 cup buffalo sauce
- 4 large flour tortillas
- 1 cup shredded cheddar cheese
- 1/2 cup blue cheese, crumbled
- Ranch dressing for dipping
- 1 lb tortilla chips
- 1 cup black beans, drained and rinsed
- 1 cup diced tomatoes
- 1 cup shredded Monterey Jack cheese
- 1/2 cup sliced black olives
- Jalapeño slices for garnish
- Sour cream for dipping

Directions:

1. Preheat one side of your Air Fryer to Air Fry at 400°F for buffalo chicken quesadillas and the other side at 375°F for loaded nacho bites.
2. In a bowl, mix shredded chicken and buffalo sauce.
3. Place one tortilla in one basket, spread a layer of buffalo chicken, sprinkle with cheddar and blue cheese, and top with another tortilla.
4. Repeat for the remaining quesadillas.
5. Air fry the quesadillas for 10 minutes, flipping halfway through, until they are crispy and the cheese is melted.
6. In the other basket, spread a layer of tortilla chips, top with black beans, diced tomatoes, Monterey Jack cheese, and sliced black olives.
7. Air fry the loaded nacho bites for 10 minutes, shaking the basket halfway

through, until the cheese is melted.
8. Press the Match Cook button.
9. Garnish nacho bites with jalapeño slices and serve with sour cream.

Nutritional Value (Amount per Serving):

Calories: 1408; Fat: 75.71; Carb: 133.89; Protein: 47.3

Pesto Stuffed Mushrooms & Balsamic Glazed Bruschetta

Prep Time: 20 Minutes   Cook Time: 15 Minutes   Serves: 4

Ingredients:

- 16 large mushrooms, stems removed
- 1 cup ricotta cheese
- 1/4 cup pesto sauce
- 1/4 cup grated Parmesan cheese
- Salt and pepper to taste
- Breadcrumbs for topping
- Baguette slices
- 2 large tomatoes, diced
- 1/2 cup fresh mozzarella, diced
- 1/4 cup fresh basil, chopped
- 2 tablespoons balsamic glaze

Directions:

1. Preheat one side of your Air Fryer to Air Fry at 375°F for pesto stuffed mushrooms and Roast at 400°F for balsamic glazed bruschetta.
2. In a bowl, mix ricotta cheese, pesto sauce, Parmesan cheese, salt, and pepper.
3. Fill each mushroom cap with the ricotta mixture and sprinkle with breadcrumbs.
4. Place the stuffed mushrooms in one basket.
5. Arrange baguette slices in the second basket.
6. Air fry the mushrooms for 15 minutes until they are golden and the filling is set.
7. Meanwhile, mix diced tomatoes, fresh mozzarella, and chopped basil in a bowl.
8. Preheat the other side of the Air Fryer to Roast.
9. Roast the baguette slices for 2-3 minutes until they are golden.
10. Press the Smart Finish button.
11. Top the toasted baguette slices with the tomato-mozzarella mixture and drizzle with balsamic glaze.

12. Serve the pesto stuffed mushrooms alongside balsamic glazed bruschetta for a delightful appetizer duo.

Nutritional Value (Amount per Serving):

Calories: 311; Fat: 20.24; Carb: 15.64; Protein: 20.12

Honey Sriracha Chicken Skewers & Teriyaki Pineapple Bites

Prep Time: 25 Minutes   Cook Time: 20 Minutes   Serves: 4

Ingredients:

- 1 lb chicken breast, cut into cubes
- 1/4 cup honey
- 2 tablespoons Sriracha sauce
- 1 tablespoon soy sauce
- 1 tablespoon sesame seeds
- Chopped green onions for garnish
- 2 cups pineapple chunks
- 1/2 cup teriyaki sauce
- 1 teaspoon sesame oil
- Wooden skewers for serving

Directions:

1. Preheat one side of your Air Fryer to Air Fry at 400°F for honey Sriracha chicken skewers and the other side at 375°F for teriyaki pineapple bites.
2. In a bowl, mix chicken cubes, honey, Sriracha sauce, soy sauce, and sesame seeds.
3. Thread the marinated chicken onto skewers and place them in one basket.
4. In another bowl, toss pineapple chunks with teriyaki sauce and sesame oil.
5. Arrange the teriyaki pineapple bites in the second basket.
6. Press the Match Cook button.
7. Air fry both baskets for 20 minutes, shaking halfway through, until the chicken is cooked and glazed, and the pineapple is caramelized.
8. Swap the baskets after 10 minutes for even cooking.
9. Garnish the chicken skewers with chopped green onions and serve with teriyaki pineapple bites on skewers.

Nutritional Value (Amount per Serving):

Calories: 369; Fat: 14.05; Carb: 58.37; Protein: 29.38

Spinach and Feta Stuffed Mushrooms &

Mediterranean Pita Chips

Prep Time: 30 Minutes   Cook Time: 15 Minutes   Serves: 4

Ingredients:

- 16 large mushrooms, stems removed
- 1 cup frozen spinach, thawed and drained
- 1/2 cup feta cheese, crumbled
- 1/4 cup cream cheese, softened
- 1/4 cup breadcrumbs
- 1/4 teaspoon garlic powder
- Salt and pepper to taste
- 4 whole wheat pita bread, cut into wedges
- 1/4 cup olive oil
- 1 teaspoon dried oregano
- 1/2 teaspoon garlic powder
- Hummus for dipping

Directions:

1. Preheat one side of your Air Fryer to Air Fry at 375°F for stuffed mushrooms and 400°F for pita chips.
2. In a bowl, mix thawed spinach, feta cheese, cream cheese, breadcrumbs, garlic powder, salt, and pepper.
3. Fill each mushroom cap with the spinach and feta mixture.
4. Place the stuffed mushrooms in one basket.
5. In another bowl, toss pita wedges with olive oil, dried oregano, and garlic powder.
6. Arrange the seasoned pita chips in the second basket.
7. Press the Match Cook button.
8. Air fry both baskets for 15 minutes, shaking halfway through, until the mushrooms are tender and the pita chips are golden and crispy.
9. Swap the baskets after 7 minutes for even cooking.
10. Serve the stuffed mushrooms with hummus and enjoy the Mediterranean pita chips on the side.

Nutritional Value (Amount per Serving):

Calories: 339; Fat: 23.69; Carb: 24.43; Protein: 11.42

Crispy Coconut Tofu Bites & Thai Peanut Zoodles

Prep Time: 35 Minutes   Cook Time: 20 Minutes   Serves: 4

Ingredients:

- 1 block firm tofu, pressed and cut into cubes

- 1/2 cup coconut milk
- 1 cup shredded coconut
- 1 cup panko breadcrumbs
- 1 teaspoon curry powder
- 1/2 teaspoon garlic powder
- Sweet chili sauce for dipping
- 4 zucchinis, spiralized
- 1/4 cup peanut butter
- 2 tablespoons soy sauce
- 1 tablespoon rice vinegar
- 1 tablespoon sesame oil
- Crushed peanuts and chopped cilantro for garnish

Directions:

1. Preheat one side of your Air Fryer to Air Fry at 375°F for coconut tofu bites and the other side at 400°F for Thai peanut zoodles.
2. In a bowl, soak tofu cubes in coconut milk.
3. In another bowl, combine shredded coconut, panko breadcrumbs, curry powder, and garlic powder.
4. Coat each tofu cube in the coconut-panko mixture.
5. Place the crispy coconut tofu bites in one basket.
6. In a bowl, whisk together peanut butter, soy sauce, rice vinegar, and sesame oil.
7. Toss spiralized zucchini in the peanut sauce.
8. Arrange the Thai peanut zoodles in the second basket.
9. Press the Match Cook button.
10. Air fry both baskets for 20 minutes, shaking halfway through, until the coconut tofu bites are golden and the zoodles are tender.
11. Swap the baskets after 10 minutes for even cooking.
12. Garnish zoodles with crushed peanuts and chopped cilantro. Serve coconut tofu bites with sweet chili sauce.

Nutritional Value (Amount per Serving):

Calories: 272; Fat: 19.93; Carb: 14.81; Protein: 11.42

Bacon-Wrapped Jalapeño Poppers & Garlic Parmesan Bread Twists

Prep Time: 30 Minutes   Cook Time: 20 Minutes   Serves: 4

Ingredients:

- 8 large jalapeños, halved and seeded
- 1 cup cream cheese, softened

- 1 cup shredded cheddar cheese
- 16 slices bacon, cut in half
- Toothpicks for securing
- 1 lb pizza dough
- 1/4 cup unsalted butter, melted
- 2 cloves garlic, minced
- 1/4 cup grated Parmesan cheese
- 1 teaspoon dried oregano

Directions:

1. Preheat one side of your Air Fryer to Air Fry at 400°F for jalapeño poppers and 375°F for bread twists.
2. In a bowl, mix cream cheese and shredded cheddar.
3. Fill each jalapeño half with the cheese mixture.
4. Wrap each jalapeño with a half-slice of bacon and secure with toothpicks.
5. Place the bacon-wrapped jalapeño poppers in one basket.
6. Roll out pizza dough and cut into strips.
7. Twist each strip and place them in the second basket.
8. In a small bowl, mix melted butter, minced garlic, Parmesan cheese, and dried oregano.
9. Brush the garlic Parmesan mixture over the bread twists.
10. Press the Match Cook button.
11. Air fry both baskets for 20 minutes, shaking halfway through, until the jalapeño poppers are crispy and the bread twists are golden.
12. Serve the bacon-wrapped jalapeño poppers with the garlic Parmesan bread twists for a delicious combination.

Nutritional Value (Amount per Serving):

Calories: 1181; Fat: 84.77; Carb: 68.64; Protein: 37.22

Caprese Stuffed Mushrooms & Italian Sausage Stuffed Peppers

Prep Time: 25 Minutes   Cook Time: 20 Minutes   Serves: 4

Ingredients:

- 16 large mushrooms, stems removed
- 1 cup cherry tomatoes, halved
- 1/2 cup fresh mozzarella balls
- 1/4 cup fresh basil, chopped
- Balsamic glaze for drizzling
- 4 bell peppers, halved and seeded
- 1 lb Italian sausage, cooked and crumbled

- 1 cup cooked quinoa
- 1 cup marinara sauce
- 1 cup shredded mozzarella cheese

Directions:

1. Preheat one side of your Air Fryer to Air Fry at 375°F for stuffed mushrooms and 400°F for stuffed peppers.
2. In a bowl, mix cherry tomatoes, mozzarella balls, and chopped basil.
3. Fill each mushroom cap with the caprese mixture.
4. Place the caprese stuffed mushrooms in one basket.
5. In another bowl, mix cooked Italian sausage, cooked quinoa, and marinara sauce.
6. Fill each bell pepper half with the Italian sausage mixture.
7. Sprinkle shredded mozzarella on top.
8. Place the stuffed peppers in the second basket.
9. Press the Match Cook button.
10. Air fry both baskets for 20 minutes, shaking halfway through, until the mushrooms are tender and the peppers are cooked through.
11. Swap the baskets after 10 minutes for even cooking.
12. Drizzle balsamic glaze over the caprese stuffed mushrooms and serve them with the Italian sausage stuffed peppers.

Nutritional Value (Amount per Serving):

Calories: 570; Fat: 33.233; Carb: 31.35; Protein: 37.88

Chapter 7: Desserts

Churro Bites with Chocolate Dipping Sauce

Prep Time: 20 Minutes   Cook Time: 10 Minutes   Serves: 4

Ingredients:

- 1 cup all-purpose flour
- 1/4 cup unsalted butter
- 1 cup water
- 1 tablespoon sugar
- 1/4 teaspoon salt
- 1 teaspoon vanilla extract
- 2 large eggs
- 1/4 cup sugar mixed with 1 teaspoon ground cinnamon (for coating)
- 1/2 cup chocolate chips
- 1/4 cup heavy cream

Directions:

1. In a saucepan, combine butter, water, sugar, and salt. Bring to a boil, then remove from heat.
2. Stir in the flour until well combined. Let the mixture cool for a few minutes.
3. Preheat one side of your Air Fryer to Air Fry at 375°F.
4. Beat in the eggs, one at a time, until the dough is smooth. Add vanilla extract and mix.
5. Transfer the churro dough to a piping bag with a star tip. Pipe small, bite-sized portions onto the Air Fryer basket.
6. Air fry for 8-10 minutes or until the churro bites are golden brown and crispy.
7. In a microwave-safe bowl, heat chocolate chips and heavy cream until melted. Stir until smooth.
8. Coat the cooked churro bites in the cinnamon-sugar mixture and serve with the chocolate dipping sauce.

Nutritional Value (Amount per Serving):

Calories: 393; Fat: 19.64; Carb: 46.67; Protein: 6.86

Lemon Blueberry Bread Pudding

Prep Time: 15 Minutes   Cook Time: 25 Minutes   Serves: 4

Ingredients:

- 4 cups cubed day-old bread (French or brioche)
- 1 cup fresh blueberries

- Zest of 1 lemon
- 1 cup milk
- 3/4 cup granulated sugar
- 3 large eggs
- 1 teaspoon vanilla extract
- 1/4 teaspoon salt
- Powdered sugar for dusting (optional)

Directions:

1. In a bowl, combine cubed bread, blueberries, and lemon zest.
2. In a separate bowl, whisk together milk, sugar, eggs, vanilla extract, and salt.
3. Preheat one side of your Air Fryer to Bake at 350°F.
4. Pour the wet mixture over the bread and blueberries. Gently stir until the bread is evenly coated.
5. Transfer the mixture into a greased baking dish that fits into the Air Fryer basket.
6. Bake for 20-25 minutes or until the bread pudding is set and golden brown on top.
7. Once done, switch the other side of the Air Fryer to Air Broil at 400°F.
8. Air broil for an additional 2-3 minutes for a crispy top.
9. Optional: Dust with powdered sugar before serving.

Nutritional Value (Amount per Serving):

Calories: 858; Fat: 11.11; Carb: 161.89; Protein: 28.78

Pineapple Coconut Crisp

Prep Time: 20 Minutes   Cook Time: 20 Minutes   Serves: 4

Ingredients:

- 2 cups fresh pineapple chunks
- 1 cup shredded coconut
- 1/2 cup granulated sugar
- 2 tablespoons cornstarch
- 1 cup old-fashioned oats
- 1/2 cup chopped nuts (macadamia or almonds)
- 1/4 cup coconut oil, melted
- Vanilla ice cream for serving (optional)

Directions:

1. In a bowl, mix pineapple chunks, shredded coconut, sugar, and cornstarch.
2. Preheat one side of your Air Fryer to Bake at 350°F.
3. In a separate bowl, combine oats, chopped nuts, and melted coconut oil.

Mix until crumbly.

4. Spread the pineapple mixture in one basket of the Air Fryer.
5. Sprinkle the oat-nut mixture evenly over the pineapple.
6. Bake for 18-20 minutes or until the topping is golden brown and the pineapple is bubbly.
7. Once done, switch the Air Fryer to Air Broil at 400°F.
8. Air broil for an additional 2 minutes for extra crunch.
9. Serve warm, optionally with a scoop of vanilla ice cream.
10. Enjoy this tropical Pineapple Coconut Crisp!

Nutritional Value (Amount per Serving):

Calories: 509; Fat: 18.75; Carb: 70.36; Protein: 7.07

Caramel Pecan Banana Foster

Prep Time: 15 Minutes   Cook Time: 15 Minutes   Serves: 4

Ingredients:

- 4 ripe bananas, sliced
- 1/2 cup chopped pecans
- 1/4 cup unsalted butter
- 1/2 cup brown sugar
- 1/4 cup dark rum (optional)
- 1 teaspoon vanilla extract
- Vanilla ice cream for serving

Directions:

1. Preheat one side of your Air Fryer to Air Fry at 375°F.
2. In a skillet over medium heat, melt butter. Add brown sugar and stir until dissolved.
3. Add sliced bananas and chopped pecans to the skillet. Cook until bananas arc softened.
4. If using rum, carefully add it to the skillet and ignite with a long lighter. Allow the flames to subside.
5. Stir in vanilla extract and cook for an additional 2 minutes.
6. Transfer the banana foster mixture to one basket of the Air Fryer.
7. Air fry for 12-15 minutes, stirring halfway through, until the bananas are caramelized.
8. Serve the caramelized bananas and pecans over vanilla ice cream.

Nutritional Value (Amount per Serving):

Calories: 461; Fat: 22.99; Carb: 57.59; Protein: 3.42

Strawberry Shortcake Skewers

Prep Time: 15 Minutes   Cook Time: 8 Minutes   Serves: 4

Ingredients:

- 2 cups fresh strawberries, hulled and halved
- 1 cup angel food cake, cut into cubes
- 1/2 cup white chocolate chips, melted
- 1/4 cup chopped mint leaves (optional)

Directions:

1. Preheat one side of your Air Fryer to Air Fry at 375°F.
2. Thread strawberry halves and angel food cake cubes onto skewers, alternating between the two.
3. Place the skewers in the Air Fryer basket.
4. Air fry for 6-8 minutes, turning halfway through, until the strawberries are softened and the cake is golden.
5. Drizzle melted white chocolate over the skewers.
6. Optional: Sprinkle chopped mint leaves for a fresh touch.
7. Remove from the Air Fryer and let them cool slightly before serving.

Nutritional Value (Amount per Serving):

Calories: 173; Fat: 7.55; Carb: 25.24; Protein: 2.57

Molten Lava Chocolate Soufflés

Prep Time: 20 Minutes   Cook Time: 10 Minutes   Serves: 4

Ingredients:

- 1 cup dark chocolate chips
- 1/2 cup unsalted butter
- 1/4 cup all-purpose flour
- 1/2 cup powdered sugar
- 3 large eggs
- 3 large egg yolks
- 1 teaspoon vanilla extract
- Pinch of salt
- Powdered sugar for dusting

Directions:

1. Preheat one side of your Air Fryer to Bake at 375°F.
2. In a microwave-safe bowl, melt chocolate chips and butter together. Stir until smooth.
3. In a separate bowl, whisk together flour, powdered sugar, eggs, egg yolks, vanilla extract, and a pinch of salt.
4. Add the melted chocolate mixture to the egg mixture and whisk until well combined.
5. Grease four ramekins and pour the batter evenly into each.
6. Place the ramekins in one basket of the Air Fryer.
7. Bake for 10 minutes or until the edges are set, but the center is still gooey.
8. Once done, switch the Air Fryer to Air Broil at 400°F.

9. Dust the tops of the soufflés with powdered sugar and air broil for an additional 1-2 minutes until golden.
10. Remove from the Air Fryer and let them cool for a few minutes before serving.

Nutritional Value (Amount per Serving):

Calories: 600; Fat: 37.87; Carb: 56.82; Protein: 8.22

Raspberry Almond Galette

Prep Time: 15 Minutes   Cook Time: 20 Minutes   Serves: 4

Ingredients:

- 1 refrigerated pie crust
- 1 cup fresh raspberries
- 1/4 cup granulated sugar
- 1/4 cup almond meal
- 1 tablespoon lemon juice
- 1 teaspoon almond extract
- 1 tablespoon sliced almonds
- 1 egg (beaten, for egg wash)
- Powdered sugar for dusting

Directions:

1. Preheat one side of your Air Fryer to Bake at 375°F.
2. Roll out the pie crust on a parchment paper-lined surface.
3. In a bowl, mix raspberries, sugar, almond meal, lemon juice, and almond extract.
4. Place the pie crust on the Air Fryer basket and spoon the raspberry mixture onto the center, leaving a border.
5. Fold the edges of the crust over the filling, creating a rustic galette shape.
6. Brush the edges of the crust with beaten egg and sprinkle sliced almonds over the top.
7. Bake for 18-20 minutes or until the crust is golden brown and the filling is bubbly.
8. Remove the galette from the Air Fryer and let it cool slightly.
9. Dust with powdered sugar before serving.

Nutritional Value (Amount per Serving):

Calories: 324; Fat: 14.99; Carb: 43.05; Protein: 5.61

Pumpkin Spice Donut Holes

Prep Time: 15 Minutes   Cook Time: 8 Minutes   Serves: 4

Ingredients:

- 1 cup canned pumpkin puree
- 1/2 cup granulated sugar

- 1/4 cup unsalted butter, melted
- 1 large egg
- 2 cups all-purpose flour
- 1 tablespoon baking powder
- 1/2 teaspoon salt
- 1 teaspoon ground cinnamon
- 1/2 teaspoon ground nutmeg
- 1/4 teaspoon ground cloves
- Vegetable oil for frying
- 1/2 cup powdered sugar (for coating)

Directions:

1. In a bowl, whisk together pumpkin puree, sugar, melted butter, and egg until smooth.
2. In a separate bowl, combine flour, baking powder, salt, cinnamon, nutmeg, and cloves.
3. Add the dry ingredients to the pumpkin mixture and stir until a soft dough forms.
4. Preheat one side of your Air Fryer to Air Fry at 375°F.
5. Using a small scoop, drop spoonfuls of the dough into the Air Fryer basket.
6. Air fry for 6-8 minutes, turning halfway through, until the donut holes are golden brown.
7. Toss the warm donut holes in powdered sugar until evenly coated.

Nutritional Value (Amount per Serving):

Calories: 501; Fat: 16.98; Carb: 80.16; Protein: 8.66

Cinnamon Apple Wonton Cups

Prep Time: 15 Minutes   Cook Time: 12 Minutes   Serves: 4

Ingredients:

- 2 cups diced apples (Granny Smith or your favorite variety)
- 2 tablespoons unsalted butter
- 1/4 cup brown sugar
- 1 teaspoon ground cinnamon
- 1 package wonton wrappers
- Cooking spray
- Whipped cream for serving (optional)

Directions:

1. In a skillet, melt butter over medium heat. Add diced apples, brown sugar, and cinnamon. Cook until apples are tender.
2. Preheat one side of your Air Fryer to Air Fry at 375°F.
3. Gently press wonton wrappers into a greased muffin tin to create cups.
4. Spoon the cooked apple mixture into each wonton cup.
5. Place the filled muffin tin in the Air Fryer basket.
6. Air fry for 10-12 minutes or until the wonton cups are golden brown and crispy.

7. Remove the muffin tin from the Air Fryer and let it cool slightly.
8. Optional: Serve with a dollop of whipped cream for extra indulgence.

Nutritional Value (Amount per Serving):

Calories: 169; Fat: 4.66; Carb: 31.23; Protein: 2.33

Mango Coconut Rice Pudding

Prep Time: 20 Minutes   Cook Time: 20 Minutes   Serves: 4

Ingredients:

- 1 cup Arborio rice
- 3 cups coconut milk
- 1/2 cup sugar
- 1 cup diced mango
- 1/4 cup shredded coconut, toasted
- 1 teaspoon vanilla extract
- Pinch of salt

Directions:

1. In a saucepan, combine Arborio rice, coconut milk, sugar, and a pinch of salt. Bring to a simmer.
2. Preheat one side of your Air Fryer to Bake at 350°F.
3. Transfer the rice mixture to a greased baking dish that fits into the Air Fryer basket.
4. Bake for 18-20 minutes or until the rice is cooked and the pudding is creamy.
5. Once done, switch the Air Fryer to Air Broil at 400°F.
6. Stir in diced mango and vanilla extract into the rice pudding.
7. Sprinkle toasted shredded coconut on top.
8. Air broil for an additional 2-3 minutes until the coconut is golden.
9. Remove from the Air Fryer and let it cool slightly before serving.

Nutritional Value (Amount per Serving):

Calories: 586; Fat: 49.25; Carb: 43.97; Protein: 8.51

Cranberry Orange Bread Pudding

Prep Time: 15 Minutes   Cook Time: 25 Minutes   Serves: 4

Ingredients:

- 4 cups cubed day-old bread
- 1 cup fresh or frozen cranberries
- Zest of 1 orange
- 1 cup milk
- 3/4 cup granulated sugar

- 3 large eggs
- 1 teaspoon vanilla extract
- 1/4 teaspoon salt
- Powdered sugar for dusting (optional)

Directions:

1. In a bowl, combine cubed bread, cranberries, and orange zest.
2. In a separate bowl, whisk together milk, sugar, eggs, vanilla extract, and salt.
3. Preheat one side of your Air Fryer to Bake at 350°F.
4. Pour the wet mixture over the bread and cranberries. Gently stir until the bread is evenly coated.
5. Transfer the mixture into a greased baking dish that fits into the Air Fryer basket.
6. Bake for 20-25 minutes or until the bread pudding is set and the top is golden brown.
7. Once done, switch the Air Fryer to Air Broil at 400°F.
8. Air broil for an additional 2-3 minutes for a crispy top.
9. Dust with powdered sugar before serving.

Nutritional Value (Amount per Serving):

Calories: 428; Fat: 6.62; Carb: 84.99; Protein: 7.5

Chocolate Peanut Butter Banana Spring Rolls

Prep Time: 20 Minutes   Cook Time: 10 Minutes   Serves: 4

Ingredients:

- 4 large spring roll wrappers
- 2 ripe bananas, sliced
- 1/4 cup creamy peanut butter
- 1/4 cup chocolate chips, melted
- Cooking spray

Directions:

1. Preheat one side of your Air Fryer to Air Fry at 375°F.
2. Lay out the spring roll wrappers and place sliced bananas in the center of each.
3. Spoon a dollop of peanut butter over the bananas.
4. Fold the sides of the wrappers and then roll them up tightly.
5. Brush the rolls with melted chocolate.
6. Place the rolls in the Air Fryer basket.
7. Air fry for 8-10 minutes or until the spring rolls are golden and crispy.
8. Remove the rolls and let them cool for a minute before serving.

Nutritional Value (Amount per Serving):

Calories: 329; Fat: 15.35; Carb: 42.07; Protein: 8.36

Blueberry Lemon Cheesecake Bars

Prep Time: 20 Minutes   Cook Time: 30 Minutes   Serves: 4

Ingredients:

- 1 cup graham cracker crumbs
- 1/4 cup unsalted butter, melted
- 1 cup cream cheese, softened
- 1/2 cup granulated sugar
- 2 large eggs
- Zest of 1 lemon
- 1 tablespoon fresh lemon juice
- 1 cup fresh blueberries

Directions:

1. In a bowl, combine graham cracker crumbs and melted butter. Press into the bottom of a greased baking dish.
2. Preheat one side of your Air Fryer to Bake at 350°F.
3. In a separate bowl, beat cream cheese, sugar, eggs, lemon zest, and lemon juice until smooth.
4. Pour the cream cheese mixture over the crust.
5. Sprinkle fresh blueberries evenly over the top.
6. Bake for 25-30 minutes or until the cheesecake is set.
7. Once done, switch the Air Fryer to Air Broil at 400°F.
8. Air broil for an additional 2-3 minutes for a golden top.
9. Remove from the Air Fryer and let them cool before cutting into bars.

Nutritional Value (Amount per Serving):

Calories: 399; Fat: 27.78; Carb: 33; Protein: 6.79

Chai Spiced Apple Hand Pies

Prep Time: 25 Minutes   Cook Time: 12 Minutes   Serves: 4

Ingredients:

- 2 cups diced apples
- 1/4 cup brown sugar
- 1 teaspoon ground cinnamon
- 1/2 teaspoon ground cardamom
- 1/4 teaspoon ground cloves
- 1 package refrigerated pie crusts
- 1/4 cup unsalted butter, melted
- Powdered sugar for dusting (optional)

Directions:

1. In a bowl, mix diced apples, brown sugar, and spices.
2. Preheat one side of your Air Fryer to Air Fry at 375°F.
3. Roll out the pie crusts and cut them into circles.

4. Spoon a portion of the apple mixture onto one half of each circle.
5. Fold the other half over the filling, sealing the edges with a fork.
6. Place the hand pies in the Air Fryer basket.
7. Air fry for 10-12 minutes or until the pies are golden brown.
8. Once done, switch the Air Fryer to Air Broil at 400°F.
9. Air broil for an additional 2 minutes for a flaky finish.
10. Dust with powdered sugar before serving.

Nutritional Value (Amount per Serving):

Calories: 409; Fat: 22.09; Carb: 51.72; Protein: 2.51

Strawberry Basil Shortcakes

Prep Time: 20 Minutes   Cook Time: 12 Minutes   Serves: 4

Ingredients:

- 2 cups fresh strawberries, sliced
- 1/4 cup granulated sugar
- 1 tablespoon fresh basil, finely chopped
- 1 package store-bought shortcakes or biscuits
- Whipped cream for serving

Directions:

1. In a bowl, combine sliced strawberries, sugar, and chopped basil. Let them macerate for 15 minutes.
2. Preheat one side of your Air Fryer to Air Fry at 350°F.
3. Place the shortcakes or biscuits on a baking sheet and warm them in the Air Fryer for 5 minutes.
4. Split the shortcakes in half horizontally.
5. Spoon the strawberry mixture over the bottom halves.
6. Place the filled shortcakes in the Air Fryer basket.
7. Air fry for 6-8 minutes or until the shortcakes are warm and slightly crispy.
8. Remove the shortcakes from the Air Fryer and top them with the other halves.
9. Serve with a dollop of whipped cream.

Nutritional Value (Amount per Serving):

Calories: 468; Fat: 16.9; Carb: 71.58; Protein: 8.5

Mint Chocolate Chip Cookie Dough Bites

Prep Time: 20 Minutes   Cook Time: 8 Minutes   Serves: 4

Ingredients:

- 1 cup edible cookie dough (store-bought or homemade)
- 1/4 cup mini chocolate chips
- 1 tablespoon fresh mint, finely chopped
- 1/4 cup powdered sugar for dusting

Directions:

1. In a bowl, mix together edible cookie dough, mini chocolate chips, and chopped mint.
2. Preheat one side of your Air Fryer to Air Fry at 375°F.
3. Using a small scoop, drop spoonfuls of the cookie dough onto the Air Fryer basket.
4. Air fry for 6-8 minutes or until the cookie dough bites are golden and slightly crispy.
5. Remove the bites and let them cool for a minute.
6. Dust with powdered sugar before serving.

Nutritional Value (Amount per Serving):

Calories: 219; Fat: 8.41; Carb: 24.31; Protein: 10.95

Mango Sticky Rice Egg Rolls

Prep Time: 30 Minutes   Cook Time: 12 Minutes   Serves: 4

Ingredients:

- 1 cup glutinous rice, soaked and cooked
- 2 ripe mangoes, peeled and diced
- 1/4 cup coconut milk
- 2 tablespoons sugar
- 1/2 teaspoon salt
- 8 spring roll wrappers
- Cooking spray
- Sesame seeds for garnish (optional)
- Coconut flakes for garnish (optional)

Directions:

1. In a bowl, mix cooked glutinous rice, diced mangoes, coconut milk, sugar, and salt until well combined.
2. Preheat one side of your Air Fryer to Air Fry at 375°F.
3. Lay out a spring roll wrapper, and spoon a portion of the mango rice mixture onto the center.
4. Fold the sides of the wrapper and then roll it up tightly. Seal the edges with a dab of water.
5. Repeat the process for the remaining wrappers.
6. Place the mango sticky rice egg rolls in the Air Fryer basket.
7. Air fry for 10-12 minutes or until the egg rolls are golden and crispy.
8. Remove the egg rolls and let them cool for a minute.
9. Garnish with sesame seeds and coconut flakes for extra flavor and presentation.

Triple Chocolate Lava Cake Delight

Prep Time: 15 Minutes   Cook Time: 12 Minutes   Serves: 4

Ingredients:

- 1 cup semisweet chocolate chips
- 1/2 cup unsalted butter
- 1/4 cup all-purpose flour
- 1/2 cup powdered sugar
- 2 large eggs
- 1 teaspoon vanilla extract
- Pinch of salt
- 1/4 cup white chocolate chips
- 1/4 cup milk chocolate chips
- Vanilla ice cream (optional, for serving)

Directions:

1. Preheat one side of your Air Fryer to Bake at 350°F and press the Smart Finish button.
2. In a microwave-safe bowl, melt semisweet chocolate chips and butter together. Stir until smooth.
3. In a separate bowl, whisk together flour and powdered sugar. Add the melted chocolate mixture to the flour-sugar mixture. Mix well.
4. Beat in the eggs, one at a time, until fully incorporated. Stir in vanilla extract and a pinch of salt. Grease four ramekins and pour the batter evenly into each.
5. Sprinkle white chocolate chips and milk chocolate chips on top of the batter in each ramekin.
6. Place the filled ramekins in one basket of the Air Fryer. Bake for 12 minutes or until the edges are set, but the center is still soft.
7. Once done, switch the Air Fryer to Air Broil at 400°F.
8. Carefully remove the ramekins and let them cool for a minute.
9. Place the ramekins in the second basket and air broil for an additional 1-2 minutes until the tops are slightly crispy.
10. Remove from the Air Fryer and let them cool for a few minutes before serving.
11. Optionally, serve warm with a scoop of vanilla ice cream for an extra indulgence.

Nutritional Value (Amount per Serving):

Calories: 536; Fat: 34.52; Carb: 57.59; Protein: 6.33

APPENDIX RECIPE INDEX

Made in United States
Troutdale, OR
12/01/2024

25624289R00064